HOW ANIL NAIK BUILT L&T'S REMARKABLE GROWTH TRAJECTORY

HOW ANIL NAIK BUILT L&T'S REMARKABLE GROWTH TRAJECTORY

R. Gopalakrishnan
Pallavi Mody

RUPA

Published by
Rupa Publications India Pvt. Ltd 2020
7/16, Ansari Road, Daryaganj
New Delhi 110002

Sales Centres:
Allahabad Bengaluru Chennai
Hyderabad Jaipur Kathmandu
Kolkata Mumbai

Copyright © R. Gopalakrishnan and Pallavi Mody 2020

The views and opinions expressed in this book are the authors own and the facts are as reported by them which have been verified to the extent possible, and the publishers are not in any way liable for the same.

All rights reserved.
No part of this publication may be reproduced, transmitted, or stored in a retrieval system, in any form or by any means, electronic, mechanical, photocopying, recording or otherwise, without the prior permission of the publisher.

ISBN: 978-93-5333-856-5

First impression 2020

10 9 8 7 6 5 4 3 2 1

The moral right of the authors have been asserted.

Printed at Parksons Graphics Pvt. Ltd., Mumbai.

This book is sold subject to the condition that it shall not, by way of trade or otherwise, be lent, resold, hired out, or otherwise circulated, without the publisher's prior consent, in any form of binding or cover other than that in which it is published.

Contents

Preface		*vii*
1.	Evolution of L&T	1
2.	Anil Naik: Breaking Ground	25
3.	Journey from a Village to the World	33
4.	L&T Adapts to Its DNA	56
5.	Power of Transformation	66
6.	Strategic Nurturing for Future Readiness	77
7.	The Naik Way	95
Epilogue		109
Appendix: Research Methodology: Shaper's 'MBA' Grid		119
Acknowledgements		133
Index		137

Preface

This book is third in a series titled 'Shapers of Business Institutions' that looks into the mindset, behaviour and actions of a 'Shaper of an Institution'. These books are neither academic nor are they anecdotal new management mantra. Management, we believe, is performing arts, rather than a science. The distinctive feature of all the books in this series is that they are co-authored by an accomplished management practitioner and a serious academician. As authors, we reflected on our real-life observations about long-lasting and value-based companies and thought through the hypotheses that we could posit from those observations. We designed a conceptual business model and validated the model through field interviews. The result can be seen in the form of these books. The series has been envisaged based on the powerful idea of 'experience before theory'. It is positioned at the intersection of practice and theory.

SHAPING A BUSINESS INSTITUTION

The theme of the series is about the shaping of good companies into business institutions. Were we to use imagery to distinguish between institutions and companies, an institution would be solid, long-lasting and structurally strong, metaphorically like Delhi's Red Fort. On the other hand, a good company would resemble a modern, convenient and practical building. Buildings may crumble or become monuments and evolve into institutions. They may become role models for others interested in converting their own buildings into institutions. The central theme of these books is to identify the factors that help businesses become institutions.

As per the Bombay Stock Exchange (BSE) data, India has about 5,000 listed companies. How many of those companies can evolve to become institutions? What does it take for such a transformation? Does it matter if more companies are shaped into institutions in India? We believe that India's economic development and job creation crucially depend on the performance of India Inc. It is important for Indian businesses to evolve into business institutions to lead the nation to higher prosperity.

In the mid-2018, a group of academics from Bharatiya Vidya Bhavan's S.P. Jain Institute of Management and Research (SPJIMR) debated ideas around this theme. There are centurion companies and groups, which we refer to as Gen-C companies. These companies bear all the hallmark characteristics of institutions. These Gen-C institutions are storied brand names such as Tata, Godrej, Birla, Bajaj and TVS—all founded about a hundred years ago and thriving to this day.

The current interest, however, lies in the search for Gen-L institutions; L standing for liberalization. The idea was to identify institutions, which were born, or which experienced exemplary growth at the time of India's liberalization in the 1990s. Such companies should have a public image that is generally free of controversy and should have been around long enough for the researchers to make a reasoned judgment. The founder or the leadership team should have shaped the group or company into a sustainable, value-based and high performing institution. It was also important for the authors that the Shaper be alive and be able to personally speak about the subject. The books in the series are not commentaries or hagiographies about the Shapers; instead, they are intended to be more about the institutions and the institutionalization of mindset, behaviour and actions.

It is important to mention that the SPJIMR team did not intend to make judgements and comparisons as juries of awards do. Rather, it was merely trying to identify some institutions, which met certain broad criteria as exemplars that provided a basis for the research—there would surely be more exemplars, not yet identified. The process followed therefore was to identify potential Gen-L institutions, get a consensus on the list among the relevant faculty group, and then write to the Shaper, inviting the group or company's participation.

This series is a joint imprint by two well-established Indian institutions—Bharatiya Vidya Bhavan's SPJIMR and Rupa Publications, India's oldest book publisher and distributor. We, the authors, and the publisher of the series hope that the reader derives both inspiration and learning from the lessons showcased by the six institutions in this series.

A BENCHMARK SHAPER

We found it instructive to recall the portrait of an established and historic institution builder that helped us validate our approach by identifying some hallmarks of an established Shaper. Andrew Carnegie,[1] the nineteenth-century steel magnate of the United States (US), would surely be regarded as the Shaper of the great steel institution, Carnegie Steel. He was a fine businessman and a true Shaper of an entire industry as he could imagine a future that few could see in the 1870s. Even a critic of Carnegie would concede that he was indeed an institution builder of his time. The rich writings by Carnegie suggest some special and relevant characteristics.

- *Virtuous impatience:* Carnegie was impatient for his country to develop fast and ahead of Britain where he had been born into and which he had left behind. He expressed his impatience to usher in a great new future through a famous line in his book *Trimphant Democracy* published in 1886, 'The old nations of the world creep on at a snail's pace; the republic thunders past with the rush of an express.' The mindset of the Shaper was that of a man in a hurry.
- *Searing, single-minded vision:* Carnegie's genius was in recognizing early on that steel would be at the centre of the world's 'real work'. Having judged steel to be the future, he also realized that to be the 'king of the era of steel', he would have to marshal all his resources. There

---

[1] Andrew Carnegie, *Autobiography of Andrew Carnegie* (Boston, New York: Houghton Mifflin Co., 1920).

was no place for distraction.

- *Institutional duty versus personal loyalty:* While building a great institution, the conflict between personal loyalty and institutional duty will inevitably arise. By the time Carnegie was 35 years old, he had become quite wealthy by the standards of the 1870s through his sheer hard work and pragmatism. Meanwhile, his early mentor and benefactor, Tom Scott had run into financial problems. Tom Scott needed financial help from Carnegie's successful company. With steely resolve, Carnegie regretted the request because he felt that he owed a duty to his current partners rather than gratitude to his old mentor. This is an admirable early form of modern corporate governance.

- *The pursuit of money:* Carnegie believed that it was a disgrace to be rich. Of course, he wanted to earn wealth, but his desire to push for progress and excellence far outweighed his desire for wealth. He deeply felt that amassing wealth was idolatry. To him, the work was important; the money was a mere consequence. Carnegie said that money could make money while work brought the glory. He respected vision but also observed that the asylums of the world are filled with people who had vision—thinking big must be accompanied by executing and concentrating all resources for the accomplishment of that task.

- *Need for approbation:* Humility is not naturally endowed among business tycoons. Carnegie needed lots of public approbation; he had a larger-than-life image that he portrayed to the world without any hesitation. There was an unbridgeable gap between the man he wanted to be and the man that the business world rewarded him for being.

ANIL NAIK AS A SHAPER

With the greatest pleasure we are presenting this book about Larsen & Toubro (L&T), and the role Anil Naik played in shaping this great company into a business institution. We do not attempt to portray Naik as resembling Carnegie, though we did stumble upon some resemblances!

L&T was started in the pre-Independence era by two Danish engineers, Henning Holck-Larsen and Søren Kristian Toubro in 1938. L&T was a well-respected business house that contributed to nation-building after Independence. However, L&T underwent a transformation to become a business institution under the leadership of Naik.

The story of L&T and Naik runs parallel, both born about eight decades ago[2]; both went through inspiring formative years and young adulthood, and both matured by taking on larger responsibilities. Naik took up the role of Chief Executive Officer (CEO) and Managing Director (MD) when both were close to celebrating their sixtieth birthday. Naik's story is fascinating because it is the journey from the shop floor to the position of an MD, CEO and chairman that transformed the organization to a leading Indian multinational company (MNC).

What did Naik do to shape the organization? His mindset and actions demonstrate lessons about how to transform the

---

[2]L&T was started by two Danish engineers in 1938, Naik was born in 1942.

enterprise. With clear thinking, he realigned the purpose of the business to 'value creation' for its stakeholders. The Shaper in Naik saw the future and planned for the long term, created capacity, and invested in state-of-the-art technology and enterprising people to transform the organization. The investment in people was critical as that was key to sustain the business over a long period.

Though Naik never defined or articulated a 'Naik Way', we think that it emerges through the story as a contender for creating new theories of leadership and management. What worked? What was the secret sauce? How did the leader evolve into a Shaper? These questions are food for thought. We believe that the contribution of Naik that shaped L&T to be among the top 10 engineering and construction companies in the world needs to be recorded. Just like the Jack Welch Way or the Toyota Way, we find 'The Naik Way' emerging as a contender for creating a theory of leadership and management.

What do Jack Welch (CEO of GE 1981-2000), Percy Barnevik (CEO of ABB 1988-96) and Larry Bossidy (CEO AlliedSignal Inc. 1991-2002 that became Honeywell International Inc.) have in common with Naik (CEO of L&T 1999-2017)? All of them have received accolades for expanding their company's revenue, profit and share price by a factor of X under their leadership and are celebrated 'value creators'. It was Naik who introduced and built the concept of value creation in the lexicon of L&T during his tenure. We find that 'The Naik Way' is also based on the simple principles of 'Focus on Value Creation', 'Future Orientation', 'Value for Values', 'Humility and Openness' and 'Work-Life Integration'.

What we want to emphasize and underline is that

successful businesses and their Shapers have time and again shown the way forward and proved that native intelligence, hard work and values are after all the way to go. The story of how Naik changed L&T's trajectory confirms the belief that stepping out of one's comfort zone, future orientation and persistence are the key to shaping institutions. What follows is the journey of L&T and Naik that reinforce our propositions about Shapers.

In Chapter 1, we look at the 'Evolution of L&T'. Danish engineers, Henning Holck-Larsen and Søren Kristian Toubro and the journey through pre-Independence, post-Independence and post-reforms and how they catered to India's economic development.

In Chapter 2, titled 'Anil Naik: Breaking Ground', we explore Naik's background and formative years that showcase the bedrock of his value system, his family.

Chapter 3, titled 'Journey from a Village to the World' examines Naik's world of work—his first job, how he entered L&T, and his meteoric rise in the company from the position of a junior engineer to the CEO and MD in L&T.

Chapter 4, titled 'L&T Adapts to Its DNA' describes how Naik saved L&T from a takeover threat and made it a company where workers became the major shareholders.

Chapter 5, titled 'Power of Transformation', shows how L&T was converted into a blue chip company and how value creation was made the core of the organization.

Chapter 6, titled 'Strategic Nurturing for Future Readiness' deals with organizational changes and capacity creation. The business leader emerges as a Shaper when he implements unprecedented changes in the organization. His attention is focused on becoming world class, developing sustainable and progressive policies and nurturing talent to take the torch further.

Chapter 7, titled 'The Naik Way' is the final chapter that sums up the qualities of the Shaper that, in turn, brought about transformation in the institution. Consciously or unconsciously, his mindset and actions were those of a Shaper. What were those? Was he a different kind of man or did he simply do things differently? What are the valuable lessons a reader can learn from the L&T story? We have tried to capture the lessons through 'The Naik Way' in this chapter.

Chapter 1

Evolution of L&T

If you can dream it, you can do it.

—Walt Disney

In the eight decades of its existence, L&T has evolved into a world-class Indian multinational business conglomerate. Today, it maintains expertise across a spectacular array of industries such as technology, engineering, construction, infrastructure projects and manufacturing. It has achieved, over time, a leadership position in all its major lines of business. This chapter brings alive the story behind the evolution of L&T by going back in time and viewing the important milestones in the journey of this company.

AN INCREDIBLE TALE OF TWO DANISH ENGINEERS

A long time ago, two young Danish engineers, Henning Holck-Larsen (1907-2003) and Søren Kristian Toubro (1906-1982), landed in British India to represent their company, F.L. Smidth & Co. of Denmark. Toubro, who was a civil engineer, arrived in 1934 to erect and commission the equipment being supplied to cement factories in India, while Holck-Larsen, a chemical engineer by profession, arrived three years later in 1937. What follows is an account of their entrepreneurial journey that laid the foundation of the mammoth organization, L&T.

At the time of the arrival of the two gentlemen, India was a British colony. Memories of hardships and unemployment at home during the Great Depression of the early 1930s was fresh in their minds. India fascinated the young Danes and they were among the few Europeans who saw here, several business opportunities for their skills. While working on projects, they observed that the demand for machinery and equipment for Indian industry was met mainly by the West. They could see that importing machinery, erecting it and setting up the plant was good business in a country that was just beginning to industrialize. However, industry in India was still rudimentary: the British had ensured that the benefits of Industrial Revolution that was reshaping the West did not percolate down to its colonies. The Indian subcontinent was mainly used as a supplier of raw material and the market for finished products by British rulers. Yet, the two realized that events such as war-time boom or the country's need for nation-building had created windows of opportunities for entrepreneurship.

Holck-Larsen and Toubro were both experimental entrepreneurs who were like agile surfers waiting for the wave and ready to ride it. They were leaders who had the intuition and skills to take advantage of those 'waves', especially when they hit the shores, taking onlookers by surprise.

The duo could feel the heat of the freedom movement and knew that when Independence would be declared, as eventually it would, the indigenous industry would offer them opportunities of a lifetime. They were astute enough to recognize the vision of 'New India' that Indian leaders Gandhi and Nehru envisaged. They felt that such an India would 'offer great opportunities to anyone with modern technological and management skills.' The entrepreneur in them caught the early signals for huge business opportunities in India.

The first step of their journey was to start a company in British India. Their idea for starting a business in India crystallized while on a holiday in Matheran, a hill station near present-day Mumbai. As they were discussing the pros and cons of a business venture, they realized that they were temperamentally different; Holck-Larsen was a risk-taker while Toubro was more conservative. They had a good laugh at the discovery of their personality differences but thought, it could be an advantage as they complemented each other. Subsequently, they decided to go ahead with their idea of starting a business venture. When their boss at F.L. Smidth asked the reason for their decision to quit, they said that they wanted to be independent and found the opportunities in India exciting. Even as their superior tried to discourage them by saying that their ideas could be illusionary, the two friends were undeterred in their decision. They were going to start operations in India.

Indeed, all they had was a dream, and the courage to dare. The young Danes started a partnership company

Larsen & Toubro in 1938, and it was the beginning of their long-term affair with India. Little did they know then that they were making this hot, humid and dusty foreign land their *karmabhoomi!*[1]

The two partners started their office in a tiny cubicle in Ballard Estate, a business district where in a few years, L&T House, the company's sprawling headquarters would be established. At the time, the office of the start-up was so small that only one of them could fit in at a time! The four-man team included a clerk and a messenger.

IN SERVICE LIES SUCCESS

The first industry the Danes tried their hand at was the dairy industry. The reason was simple—they knew the suppliers of dairy equipment in their home country who were eager to sell their apparatus. Denmark, that was a dairying nation, had developed some unique machinery—butter churners, cream separators, pasteurizers and refrigeration machinery. The Federation of Danish Industries gave them a modest retainer and also a sales commission. L&T needed to find customers for this equipment in India. While learning the ropes of the business, Holck-Larsen and Toubro realized that they were not in a typical sales and installation job. They needed to educate their customers, provide quick and quality aftersales services, including maintenance. 'Find a potential customer and walk along for the technology transfer' was the key to their success in the dairy industry. This was the winning

---

[1] Karkaria Bachi, *The Power of E: Seven Decades of Larsen & Toubro* (L&T, 2010).

formula that later evolved into L&T's motto—In Service Lies Success. Both partners knew that customer confidence needed to be built through systematic and conscious effort. This has remained L&T's core value even after 80 years, and its willingness to serve society is a distinguishing characteristic of the organization.

For the business leader, the economy is embedded in society, and business decisions must be grounded in a socially constructed view of the world and motivated by social concerns.[2] People relations for the Shaper emerge out of respect, sensitivity and empathy for the needs of customers which leads to his engagement with the people. (See Appendix Table I for SPJIMR Shaper's Mindset–Behaviour–Action Grid). It is this central idea that helped the young Danes to transform obstacles into opportunities, starting with World War I.

Just a year after the birth of the new company, Hitler invaded Poland in 1939, and World War II broke out. Germans working in India were declared enemies by the British Raj. All foreigners, except British and Americans, were suspect. The Danes got a reprieve because the Scandinavian countries had declared neutrality. But when the German army marched into Denmark and Norway, imports from those countries were also banned. L&T found itself in a difficult spot as machinery and equipment imports from Denmark came to a standstill. L&T had to think of something new, or shut down.

Holck-Larsen and Toubro were somewhat depressed and worried until one evening, while taking stock of the machinery

---

[2]Rosabeth Moss Kanter and Rakesh Khurana, 'Advanced Leadership Note: Institutional Perspectives on Managing and Leading,' Harvard Business School Organizational Behavior Unit Case No. 410-076.

in the warehouse, they had a Eureka moment. 'If we cannot replenish the machinery by fresh imports, we need to replicate it!' Just as the ancient proverb, 'Necessity is the mother of invention', the duo had found a way out of their predicament. They dismantled the machinery, made moulds and ensured that local vendors in Bombay's Kumbharwada (present-day Dharavi) area cast them to exacting specifications. They devoted all their energy to replicating the machinery. Engineering and innovation were the two pillars on which the partners took their first baby steps. After machining, grinding and polishing, the churns, separators and pasteurizers were reassembled with their brand new indigenized parts. The machines worked! 'Bravo! We did it!' the engineers remarked with many sighs of relief. Using clones of Danish compressors, L&T added ice factories and refrigeration plants to its manufacturing line. These products proved to be a success, and L&T came to be recognized as a reliable fabricator with high standards of quality. Their smart hard work paid off as they got new orders along with precious goodwill of 'reputation of reliability'. By this time, without any fanfare, L&T as a company had graduated from a trading company to a manufacturing company. This was a big achievement for L&T as British companies such as Greaves Cotton and Alstom were still trading companies then.

Meanwhile, the war was spreading fast. Germany had invaded 11 European countries. As a result, Britain and France declared war on Germany. Within days the British dependencies—India, Australia, New Zealand, Canada and South Africa—were also drawn into the war. Wartime presented new opportunities for L&T, and the engineering duo was quick to spot these and convert them into businesses.

The first opportunity that knocked on their door was to repair and refit the war-struck ships. When the Royal Navy approached L&T for ship repair work, the Danish duo was ready to venture into this hitherto unchartered area. They seized the opportunity to refit a captured Italian ship MV Hilda, and with the help of authorities converted it into a floating workshop. The Royal Navy suggested that they could also help in degaussing[3] the ships. The business was brisk. They employed some 200-odd workers on the ship, and formed a new company, Hilda Ltd, with a well-known Parsi entrepreneur and philanthropist Sir Jamsetjee Jeejeebhoy as chairman and both Holck-Larsen and Toubro as directors. Indeed, the seeds of diversification of the company were sown during war time—from dairy equipment to shipbuilding. Who could predict then that many years hence, L&T would build war ships, submarines, offshore patrol vessels and floating docks!

The second opportunity was to install the soda ash plant for Tata. Originally, German engineers were hired by Tata to install the plant. However, wartime suspicion led British India authorities to detain these German engineers. As an alternative, Sir Homi Mody, the then director of the Tata Group, persuaded the Tata Board to give the contract for erecting the plant to the young Danes. The Tatas agreed to replace the German engineers with Danish engineers.

---

[3]Degaussing refers to the neutralization of the magnetic field of a ship by encircling it with a conductor carrying electric currents. This was used extensively in World War II by the Allies to protect their ships against the magnetic mines deployed by the Germans.

The Tata plant was then located at Mithapur in Gujarat, about 1,000 km from Bombay (now Mumbai). It could be reached by taking a long overnight train. Although Europeans in India travelled by the prestigious and expensive 'first class' of the railways, the Danish duo, who were scarce on resources at the time, travelled most of the long journey by the cheaper 'third class' coach. But, in the last lap of their journey, they upgraded their seats to arrive 'first class' in order to impress their hosts, waiting for them at Mithapur station! They were fast learning the cultural nuances of doing business in India.

Subsequently, L&T entered yet another new domain of construction projects, and set up a new company, Engineering and Construction Corporation (ECC), in 1944. There is an interesting backstory to this episode. A Danish civil engineer, Gerhard Berg, was working in Iran. He had escaped the detention camp and walked to Mumbai to see his countrymen and persuaded them to employ him. Holck-Larsen spotted a good civil engineer in Berg. L&T followed a simple principle, 'If you have the right man for a business, start the business.' And, so, the seeds of yet another diversification were sown and ECC became a towering giant with its footprints in India and the world. ECC is responsible for building many of the country's prized landmarks such as high-rise towers, airports, IT parks, metros, and roads and flyovers.

The fourth business opportunity came from several corners, and L&T responded by expanding its expertise from manufacturing dairy equipment to machinery for the consumer goods industry. Rapidly, L&T was becoming the one-stop shop for all kinds of capital goods required for industries such as hydrogenated oils, biscuits, soaps and glass. Although L&T chose to manufacture the machines that produced a large number of consumer goods, it deliberately stayed away from producing consumer goods. It was the beginning of a conscious strategy, which L&T has followed through the years.

When L&T signed an agreement with Caterpillar Tractor Company, USA, for marketing earth-moving equipment in 1945, World War II had just ended. A large number of war-surplus Caterpillar equipment was available at attractive prices. They thought of grabbing this opportunity, though the finances required were beyond the capacity of the partners. During this period, Holck-Larsen also had an opportunity to meet Mangaldas Desai, an experienced Indian lawyer at the time. Holck-Larsen spoke about the company's future prospects with such strong conviction that the astute elite instantly bought his idea. He felt that 'Holck-Larsen was a good man—a man we can trust.' Although L&T's balance sheet was not yet robust, Mangaldas Desai's decision to buy a stake in L&T was based on intuition and faith. In February 1946, Larsen & Toubro Private Limited was incorporated. It was the beginning of the long relationship of L&T with the Desai family.

PARTNERING INDEPENDENT INDIA'S GROWTH STORY

The second phase of L&T's journey was initiated with the big opportunity of supporting nation-building in Independent India. By 1947, L&T had established itself as a company rooted in India. The company bore a Danish name, but it was wholly an Indian company in equity, emotion and inspiration. The future was yet unchartered. Holck-Larsen and Toubro were comfortable and enthusiastic about further building their nascent Indian business, a journey that had begun nine years earlier. They affirmed their undivided commitment to India. The country was free and Independent, raring to grow—and so were they. They had the will, skill and resources to help build the nation. Their mission was broader than a private company driven solely by the profit motive.

India's political leadership adopted a model of a mixed economy, an amalgam of socialism and capitalism. The leaders at that time resorted to planned economic development where specific roles were assigned to the public and private sector.

The Industrial Policy Resolution 1948 segregated industries into four broad categories. First, the central government would have an absolute monopoly over three industries—arms and ammunition (defence), atomic energy and railways. Second were the industries for which only the government could set up new units. These were coal, shipbuilding, and iron and steel. The third category included 18 industries such as sugar, power, cement, textiles and automobiles. For these, the government would control total supply through licensing of capacity. Fourth and last, the private sector was free to operate in the remaining domains. L&T played a key role in India's planned economic development as they made all kinds of machines in all these categories. They became partners in India's growth story by providing strong technological support.

L&T expanded in metros, set up offices in Calcutta (now Kolkata), Madras (now Chennai) and New Delhi. Bombay (now Mumbai) remained the headquarters from where they expanded their manufacturing facility. In 1948, the company acquired 55 acres of undeveloped marsh and jungle land in Powai, Mumbai, to accommodate its growing business. A previously uninhabitable swampland subsequently became the site of L&T's main manufacturing hub. The service station, set up to service L&T's international partner in earth-moving equipment, Caterpillar Tractors, was shifted to Powai in 1950.

The year 1950 was also a turning point in the history of the company. L&T became a Public Limited Company with a paid-up capital of ₹20 lakh. The sales turnover in that year was ₹1.09 crore. The shares of the company were publicly listed.

CHURNING INDIA'S WHITE REVOLUTION[4]

L&T's association with dairy equipment remained at the core of their activities in the early 1950s. They reverted to selling imported butter churns, cream separators and pasteurizers after Independence as there was no clear industrial policy in place. However, history repeated itself when the Government of India banned imports under its import substitution policy, and L&T was quick to resort to indigenous production. The process of substituting imports with indigenization was tried and tested during wartime. L&T developed and mastered indigenous manufacturing of dairy equipment and refrigeration plants.

When Dr Verghese Kurien took up the challenging

---

[4]Operation Flood started the White Revolution in India and made the country self-sufficient in milk through the co-operative movement started by V. Kurien.

experiment of setting up Amul Dairy, a milk co-operative in Gujarat's Kaira district, L&T emerged as the best choice for supply of equipment. L&T not only supplied dairy equipment but also erected the piping and insulation machinery for the gigantic dairy. The subsequent success of Amul Dairy transformed lives of rural dairy farmers like never seen before. Amul Dairy successfully connected a large number of rural milk producers with urban consumers at a reasonable price. The Danish duo was happy and satisfied as they witnessed the success of the Amul experiment.

Going back to the Shaper's Mindset-Behaviour-Action Grid, what was on display here was their 'People Relations' and 'Stakeholder Orientation' as they were sensitive to the needs of their customers and understood the needs of the community. The L&T tagline 'People are our prime movers' that was born much later captured this sentiment of the entrepreneurial Danes. The success of Amul Dairy was later replicated in Mumbai's Worli Dairy, set up by Government of Maharashtra with aid from the United Nations Children's Fund (UNICEF).

L&T was also the key stakeholder when National Dairy Development Board (NDDB) started its Operation Flood project. This was a countrywide movement for a White Revolution by forming a national milk grid over the next three decades. The idea was to serve towns and cities with fresh milk and ensure remunerative prices for dairy farmers by eliminating intermediaries. By providing the technical know-how and machinery, L&T played a pivotal role in setting up dairies across the length and breadth of the country. Whether there was a need for storing milk in massive vertical silos, setting up massive milk pasteurizers and cream separators, building milk pipelines or even tankers for transporting milk, L&T provided solutions and technical expertise. The company that began by selling dairy equipment had made its way to become the most sought after business house, contributing immensely to Operation Flood, which eventually grew to establish India as the world's largest producer of milk.

ROOTING FOR INDIA'S GREEN REVOLUTION[5]

Almost concurrent with the White Revolution, the country was also preparing for a Green Revolution to augment domestic foodgrain production. But, unlike its core competence with dairy equipment, L&T did not have any definite advantage to support India's Green Revolution. However, India was a food-deficient economy for the first two decades of its Independence, and Indian agriculture remained traditional even when other sectors of the economy were modernizing. This led to the initiation of the Green Revolution that had a lasting impact on India's food security, and for the first time traditional agriculture used imported industrial inputs such as fertilizers, pesticides and farm machinery under the government's Intensive Agricultural Development Programme (IADP) in 1966-69. The success of this experiment and record increase in food production was hailed as the Green Revolution.

---

[5]The Green Revolution in India refers to a period when Indian agriculture adopted modern methods and technology such as the use of high yielding variety (HYV) seeds, tractors, irrigation facilities, pesticides and fertilizers. It was mainly founded by M.S. Swaminathan.

Buoyed by its success, the next challenge facing the government was to substitute imported fertilizers and pesticides by domestic production. It turned to none other than L&T to carry out this task of utmost national priority. L&T supported the policy initiative by the government to set up large-scale fertilizer plants, such as the Gujarat Narmada Valley Fertilizers Corporation (GNFC), National Fertilizers Ltd (NFL) and Rashtriya Chemicals and Fertilizers (RCF). Over the next decade, the IADP was expanded to cover many more parts of the country, and increased use of fertilizers helped India become a food-sufficient economy.

FACILITATING GROWTH OF CORE INDUSTRIES

Given the aspirations of the new nation, L&T catered to the needs of core industries for supply of machinery and equipment for steel, cement and power (including atomic energy) plants as well as fertilizer, food processing, refining and mining industries that were coming up in the country, as laid down in the Five Year Plans. L&T had already carved out a niche for itself as a leading contractor in the Capital Goods Sector.

Import substitution was the new mantra of Independent India's industrial policy. L&T obtained the licences and permits to produce the machinery and equipment indigenously. To meet the demand for plant and equipment for India's steel mining, chemical, oil and paper industries, L&T set up Utkal Machinery Limited in collaboration with three West German firms in 1960: first, GHH, a world-wide supplier of plant and equipment for the iron and steel industry; second, J.M. Voith,

Europe's largest manufacturers of pulp and papermaking machinery; and third, Heinrich Koppers, a global giant in the construction of coal refining and by-product plants. Utkal Machinery Limited, or Utmal, was set up near Rourkela in Orissa (now Odisha). L&T also supplied various sophisticated equipment for Bhilai, Bokaro, Rourkela and IISCO steel plants. With the successful completion of these jobs, L&T emerged as the largest construction contractor in the country.

The role of steel in building the nation is often compared to the spine, whereas the role of cement is a metaphor for strength. L&T was ready to take the next step after setting up several steel plants. In 1965, it acquired a licence to manufacture plant and machinery for the cement industry. When it came to the question of the cement plant, the first recourse for the Danish duo was naturally F.L. Smidth. Holck-Larsen and Toubro had neither forgotten their roots nor their reason for being in India. They had come to India nearly three decades ago to erect and commission the equipment supplied to cement factories by this same company. In technical collaboration with F.L. Smidth & Co., L&T ventured into the domain of making cement machinery at Powai.

In these ways and more, L&T literally shaped India. By fabricating steel and other metals into various shapes, sizes and forms, they made factories and machinery. By using cement, L&T gave shape to buildings and infrastructure in the country. L&T's switchgear division also played a crucial role in power distribution at the plant level and for agricultural applications. Electric power comes from the generating station at a high voltage. It is distributed to the different parts of industrial plants via low-tension switchgear. L&T customized the entire paraphernalia including switchboards, circuit breakers, power control centres and distribution panels for each industry. Competing against British and German manufacturers, L&T won important projects. The switchgear division became one of the biggest forces in the field in India due to its superior R&D, custom-designing, manufacturing, marketing and aftersales services for several industrial plants.

L&T GOES GLOBAL

Another L&T subsidiary, ECC, that was set up before Independence undertook civil construction projects and gave wings to L&T's flight. This construction division had its first international experience when they worked as sub-contractor to the Japanese Construction Consortium (JCC) in 1976. This experience of working with the Japanese allowed ECC to become thoroughly professional, especially in terms of quality and timelines, and they were able to successfully undertake the complex construction assignment of the Abu Dhabi International Airport. What followed was a series of international assignments; for example, construction of large football stadiums with a capacity of 25,000 in Iraq and Qatar, besides complex projects in Kuwait, Sri Lanka, Malaysia and the USSR. Each project took ECC further up the learning curve and value chain. ECC had spin-off benefits for its Indian projects too. The tradition of both contributing to and learning from international projects continued with other projects built by ECC not just in West and South Asia, but also Central and Southeast Asia, Russia, Africa and the Indian Ocean islands. Yet another feather was added to L&T's cap with its foray into the Middle East when it started a manufacturing complex, comprising the Modular Fabrication Yard and heavy engineering manufacturing facility in Sohar, Oman.

L&T played a critical role in the development of a large number of industries such as cement, fertilizers, power, switchgear, food processing, construction—all which have built India and made India proud. Its tagline at the time 'We make the things that make India proud', truly reflected its organizational culture. Over the years, L&T reversed the old assumption that hi-tech equipment could flow only from the West to the East. L&T has taken its polypropylene reactors to the US, desalination machinery to France and specialized reactors to the United Kingdom (UK).

L&T's anthem is as much about India as it is about the company because nationalist sentiments have been part of the company's genetic code. The founders of L&T had decided right from the beginning that they would place national interest above commercial interests. This is the reason L&T was among the first private sector companies to be involved in the vital, if less profitable, strategic areas of defence, nuclear power and space research. The participation of L&T in nation-building was summed up in Holck-Larsen's comment, 'If not L&T, who else?'

In 1976, Holck-Larsen was awarded the Magsaysay Award for International Understanding in recognition of his contribution to India's industrial development. Unfortunately, Holck-Larsen had to retire from the role of Chairman following a change in the Foreign Exchange Regulation Act (FERA) rules in India in 1978. The rules prevented foreigners from holding executive positions in India. This was perhaps the beginning of the end of foreign management in L&T since Toubro had retired much earlier in 1963. Later, however, Holck-Larsen was appointed Chairman Emeritus with an advisory role in the company.

Since its inception, L&T has been a nation builder, choosing to be in those businesses that served the country's goals. In fact, even in the decades that followed, the company grew into an engineering major under the guidance of leaders such as N.M. Desai, S.R. Subramaniam, U.V. Rao, S.D. Kulkarni and A.M. Naik.

L&T DARES TO VENTURE INTO DNA

To dare to venture into new areas became part of L&T's DNA (Defence, Nuclear, Aerospace), figuratively and literally, though it may not have happened in the same sequence.

L&T was associated with the Bhabha Atomic Research Centre (BARC) in India's nuclear programme in 1966. Dr Homi Bhabha, then chairman of BARC, approached L&T to fabricate critical components for atomic reactors for India's nuclear power plant. 'L&T's Heavy Engineering Division (HED) contributed significantly to India's nuclear programme and the development of nuclear power plants at Tarapur, Kota, Narora and Kalpakkam,' Naik revealed. Most of India's nuclear reactors were made by L&T that was involved in 18 out of 22 nuclear reactors in India.

L&T also participated in the Satellite Launch Vehicle

Programme (SLVP) under the Indian Space Research Organisation (ISRO), an organization founded and led by noted scientist Vikram Sarabhai. ISRO chose L&T as its manufacturing partner in 1970, and when ISRO launched its space programme, Naik was manager-in-charge of the manufacturing process at the time. Later, participation in India's SLVP brought the company into close contact with Abdul J. Kalam, who was then project director at ISRO. L&T constructed the launch systems and also made critical components.

In 1985, L&T also entered into a partnership with the Defence Research and Development Organisation (DRDO). Although L&T could not manufacture defence equipment because defence belonged to the restricted category, tagged 'government only', the government did seek inputs in design and development from private players like L&T. Once the drawings were done, L&T had to hand over the design to DRDO. The manufacturing of defence equipment was left to the government undertaking. Eventually, when the defence sector opened up, the government changed its policy to allow participation of the private sector for manufacturing defence equipment. L&T naturally had an advantage since they were already involved in the design and development of defence equipment. It was preferred due to its long-standing association with DRDO.

LEAD PERFORMER IN POST-REFORMS PERIOD

It was in response to a macroeconomic crisis in 1991 that India started to liberalize, privatize and globalize. The new industrial policy liberalized businesses from the licensing system, the Monopolies and Restrictive Trade Practices (MRTP) Act and the obnoxious tax structure. Privatization meant opening of several sectors hitherto reserved only for the government. To globalize the economy, the government dismantled FERA, lowered tariffs and allowed foreign investment in several sectors. The Indian economy went through a paradigm shift. The policy framework that had so far tilted towards socialism recognized the importance of capitalism for efficiency and the role of market mechanism. The economy, industry and businesses that enjoyed protection from the global competition were thrown to the world of global competition for agility and competitiveness.

There was an air of optimism in the country. The forecast for the Indian economy, starting with a BRICS report by Goldman Sachs, had placed India in the same bracket as China as the next big economy.

As always, L&T swiftly responded to the positive economic reforms by transforming itself from being a government contractor to becoming a government partner, ready to play a vital role in building a 'new India' preparing for the twenty-first century.

MAKING THE IMPOSSIBLE POSSIBLE

L&T took the reforms in stride, both as a challenge and an opportunity, to grow into new areas. As the winds of privatization blew into the country, the infrastructure sector that was reserved for the public sector so far, opened up. The scope of L&T's operations in this sector further increased.

The leadership at the company was in a position to leverage the strength that the company had built over the years. With the Indian economy, like the proverbial elephant set free to dance, L&T was the lead performer.

What L&T had been doing for the past four decades was a preparation for the horizons that economic liberalization had opened up to them. Economic reforms allowed Indian industries to bat like never before, and bowl over an incredulous world, but the playing field was not quite level. The reduction in import duties on capital goods under pressure from the World Trade Organization (WTO) meant that L&T was also competing in the domestic market with global players. But, the company swiftly learnt to devise value engineering to pare down costs at every stage to improve competitiveness. Darwin was never more relevant than what was observed in the world of business—it was truly the 'survival of the fittest'. To remain fit, businesses had to 'transform'—a process far more evolved than 'change'.

Earlier, L&T had aimed and succeeded at being the best in the country. It was following Jack Welch's famous dictum of being in the top three in any business it was engaged in. 'That's not enough!' declared A.M. Naik, who took over as CEO and MD in 1999. 'We have to be No. 1 in India and among the top three internationally.' L&T stopped being just a major engineering and equipment producing company; it scaled up into management of entire projects.

L&T was well placed to take on the opportunities that were thrown open by Public Private Partnership (PPP) in infrastructure development. Build Operate Transfer (BOT) or Build Own Operate Transfer (BOOT) created PPPs in areas of roads, bridges, airports, water supply and power. The significant shift was that L&T moved from executing government contracts to being a partner in national endeavour. It continued to make critical equipment and entire plants as well as take up projects on Engineer, Procure, Construct (EPC) or Lump Sum Turn Key (LSTK). This dramatic shift in the operations of L&T began with its first bypass road in Tamil Nadu, which it financed, built, ran and undertook toll collection until the concession period was over.

When the Vajpayee government announced the Golden Quadrilateral project to connect the four major metros—Delhi, Kolkata, Chennai and Mumbai—L&T was at the forefront, executing important road segments on BOT basis. L&T also did important segments of the prestigious Mumbai-Pune Expressway, India's first six-lane concrete expressway to globally benchmarked standards. L&T built major ports such as Dhamra in Odisha, Kattupali in Tamil Nadu and Kachchigarh in Gujarat. Even for new airport development in India, L&T had all the solutions—from runway to control tower to customer movement. In fact, L&T has developed new international airports for important Indian cities of Delhi, Mumbai, Bengaluru and Hyderabad.

L&T had perfected the art of completing projects before time by working backwards on the schedules. There was typical military precision in planning and execution. L&T was not a lazy monopoly that would cringe at the name of competition. The company adapted to the new environment with open arms and an open mind. It catered to India's infrastructural needs and expanded over time to step out as the winner on one hand and help build the nation on the other.

For example, ISRO's Polar Satellite Launch Vehicle (PSLV) and the role that L&T played with regard to it, speaks volumes about the development of in-house capabilities. Naik said in an interview, 'In February 2017, when 104 satellites weighing 1,378 kg were launched from a single rocket, PSLV-C37, our contribution was critical. We made key sections of the rockets as well as the launch platforms.' It was a technological marvel as all along the atmospheric flight, the heat shields in advanced composites protected the satellites. The solar array deployment devices enabled unfurling of the satellites when deployed. The instrumentation radars helped to know the actual position of the satellites in deployment and helped maintain orbit while the Deep Space Network communication antennae brought in data from the space probes back to the control centres on Earth.

Former Finance Minister P. Chidambaram acknowledged L&T's role in nation-building and described it as 'India's only National Sector Company,' at a grand function celebrating L&T's seventieth year and Holck-Larsen's birth centenary on 21 December 2007. He spoke of the company's contribution as '...making the impossible possible...this is an example of entrepreneurship and the ability and the confidence to chart the most difficult frontiers of business.'[6] Coining an economic classification, he stated, '[L&T] is the company of the people of India.' Here, he was referring specifically to its ownership, which is neither private nor government.

Following this narrative to recognize the contribution of the founders in building this mammoth organization, we

---

[6] Bachi Karkaria, 'The Power of E': Seven Decades of Larsen & Toubro Published in 2010 by Corporate Communication Department of L&T, pp.4–5.

return to the subject of this book—Anil Naik, the man who 'shaped' L&T. But first, we shall explore Naik's background and the influences on his formative years that shaped him. How did Naik's youth contribute to the nationalist spirit and values of his life?

Chapter 2

Anil Naik: Breaking Ground

Be the change you wish to see in the world.

—Mahatma Gandhi

The stories of L&T and Anil Naik run almost analogous. L&T was born in 1938; Naik in 1942. Both went through inspiring formative years and matured to take on greater responsibilities to initiate the changes they wished to see in the world. The young Anil Naik was inspired by Mahatma Gandhi, the father of the nation, whose life story and philosophy was for him food for thought and a basis for action.

Anil was born in south Gujarat in June 1942—the year that is etched in the collective consciousness of Indians as the time when the struggle for freedom from two hundred years of British Rule had reached its pinnacle. Gandhi confronted the British authorities with an ultimatum to Quit India, a mantra to end British Rule. The first call to Quit India was sounded at the Gowalia Tank Maidan (now August Kranti Maidan), in present-day Mumbai in August 1942, a time when freedom looked closer and more certain than ever before.

Anil's father had attended the 1942 meeting at Gowalia Tank Maidan where Gandhi demanded that the British 'Quit India', a slogan that was chanted by thousands of people. Gandhi's fearlessness charged Anil's father who was deeply touched by his philosophy.

We begin with an account of Anil's formative years in the village,[7] starting with his childhood days onwards to his world of work. The early influencing factors of his life include family culture, his schooling in a Gujarati-medium village school followed by an engineering degree from a college in Gujarat—all these helped him imbibe leadership lessons and values of fair play, justice and righteousness which remained deeply ingrained in his psyche.

As a child, Anil was nurtured by a family that was mainly engaged in education. His parents, Manibhai and Maniba, were Anavil Brahmins, a community known for its devotion to higher values in life. His grandfather, Nichchhabhai Naik, an educationist who ran a *gurukul*,[8] greatly influenced Anil. Nichchhabhai was so proficient in maths that he could mentally multiply seven-digit numbers. People were so in awe of his prowess that they would gather to watch him perform mental maths. Anil would also be part of this crowd and felt proud of his grandfather's feats. He admired his grandfather and loved the adulation he received from the people. Years later, the government recognized the

---

[7] Minhaz Merchant, *The Nationalist* (New Delhi: Harper Collins, 2017).
[8] A *gurukul* (also spelt gurukula or gurukulam) was a type of education system in ancient India with *shishya*, meaning students or disciples, living near or with the guru, in the same house.

contribution of his grandfather towards education and awarded him a gold medal. Anil remembers how proud he felt when they went to receive the gold medal at Baroda (now Vadodara), Gujarat.

At a young age, Anil learnt the importance of competence and efficiency. Perhaps, the seeds of becoming *nayak*[9] were sown in his mind through appreciation of his grandfather's life of running a *gurukul* at the grass roots level to serve the community. Nichchhabhai's life, his values and his competence deeply impacted both his son Manibhai and his grandson Anil. Anil's role model was his father Manibhai, who was inspired by Gandhi and actively participated in the freedom struggle. After Independence, Manibhai took up a job as a teacher in a school in Bombay, where the family lived a decent middle-class life.

However, destiny had something else in store for the family. Manibhai was invited to join as a principal at an upcoming school at Kharel, his native place, in the state of Gujarat. Gandhi's statement 'India lives in villages' resonated in Manibhai's mind. He was fully charged and overwhelmed by the opportunity. He felt that it was a signal from God that had created this opportunity. He cherished the idea that, like his father, he too would work at the grass roots level towards building a strong India.

Indeed, pursuing and imparting education ran in Anil's family. Some 12 or 14 professional teachers were a part of the extended family. As a result, the family was called 'Master Kutumb'.[10] Naik would proudly recount in his later years that

---
[9]Nayak refers to a heroic leader.
[10]Master Kutumb is a family of teachers.

'if you combine the teaching contribution of my father and grandfather, it would be 120 years of teaching!'

SOWING SEEDS OF LEADERSHIP

Anil was just 10 years old when the family moved to the village. He got his lessons on dedication, devotion and commitment at this tender age both from his father and his life experiences at the village. Anil's education started in a Gujarati school, where all subjects including science, history, geography and mathematics were taught in Gujarati. In those days, schools in Indian villages did not have many facilities such as tables or benches for the students. Instead, the children would sit on a floor plastered with cow dung. By modern standards, village schools even today are considered quite rudimentary, but back in those days, conditions were almost primitive. It is perhaps these factors that motivated Naik to work towards improving school facilities later in his life.

Despite these apparent inconveniences, Anil was at home in the school. He was brilliant and bubbly, and never struggled to learn his lessons. His father encouraged him to get selected as a monitor so he could imbibe leadership qualities. Anil was a conscientious child and would own up to his mistakes and resolve minor issues faced by the children in his class. So, it is evident that Anil learned to take up responsibility since childhood. At a tender age, the seeds of leadership, problem solving, decision making, accountability and responsibility were sown in Anil's mind. This confirms the adage that the best leadership training is born in the dark alleys of personal hardship and experiences.

The leadership qualities that one imbibes in childhood may seem simple, but they are of great value. Most people in adulthood struggle when they find themselves facing challenging situations in leadership roles. Instead of taking up responsibility, people with insecurities may resort to tactics of playing safe, passing the buck and indecisiveness. Perhaps, the transition from a worker to a manager to a leader was a natural progression for Naik due to his early exposure to tough situations and development of leadership qualities in an environment that valued fair play and ethics.

A FAMILY IMPARTS VALUES

Anil was close to his parents. The family had high standards of ethics and Dharma, and lived up to these lofty principles. They lived a simple life and tried to tread the right path. His father would talk to him about the great Indian epics—Ramayana[11] and Mahabharata.[12] He would quote from the Bhagavad Gita[13] to find solutions to the dilemmas in life. In addition to these, there was the all-pervasive influence of Mahatma Gandhi and his philosophy that influenced the young boy. Some of

---

[11]Composed in the fifth century BCE, the Ramayana is an ancient Indian epic about the exile and then return of Rama, prince of Ayodhya. It was originally composed in Sanskrit by the sage, Valmiki.

[12]Mahabharata is also a Sanskrit epic poem of ancient India. It is an important source of information on the development of Hinduism between 400 BCE and 200 CE, and is regarded by Hindus as both a text about dharma (Hindu moral law) and a historical document.

[13]Bhagavad Gita (often referred to as the Gita), is a 700-verse Sanskrit scripture that is part of the Hindu epic Mahabharata. The Gita is set in a narrative framework of a dialogue between the Pandava prince Arjuna and his guide and charioteer Krishna about how to lead life on the right path.

the ideals of the value system that Anil imbibed early in his life are reflected in well-known proverbs such as 'There is no substitute for hard work'; 'You don't have to be afraid of anyone when you are right'; and 'Be true'. The rapport that the father and son built during Anil's formative years was so strong that it continued to guide him on the right path even later in life.

For instance, an interesting episode from Anil's later life substantiates the value system of the Naik family. After his father's retirement, Anil's parents had come to live with him in Bombay. By then, Anil was clearly on his way up the corporate ladder. His father noticed that the family bought groceries from a nearby shop and settled the bill at the end of the month. After observing the process for a month or two, one day he said, 'The grocery bill is around ₹3,000 a month. That small shop is giving us the goods on credit even though financially we are much better off than him. Why don't we pay him ₹3,000 in advance and let him deduct as we buy?' How many of us can claim to be sensitive about the kind of credit we take from small vendors?

These values played a key role in guiding Anil—and the future of L&T—and whenever Anil found himself in a dilemma, he would imagine having a dialogue with his father and this invariably helped him find the right solution.

To conclude his school education, Anil went to the nearby city of Bilimora to write his SSC Board Examinations. Here, he stayed with relatives. Most Indian children, perhaps fearful of the outcome, are tense before examinations. But, not Anil. His relatives were surprised as he was neither nervous nor anxious; instead, he was playful. Another curious thing they observed about Anil was that he watched a Hindi film every evening. Interestingly, the exam timing from 3 p.m. to 6 p.m. was overlapping with the movie timings from 6 p.m. to 9 p.m. But, Anil's creative mind found a solution around the rule that a student could not leave the exam hall in the last 10 minutes before the exam concluded. Anil always submitted his paper about 12 minutes before the bell rang to declare 'last 10 minutes left', and he was able to beat the rule and reach in time for the movie! What's more, he cleared his SSC Board examination with good marks—the first proof of his self-confidence and intellect.

Looking at his son's academic record and aptitude, Manibhai felt that engineering would be a suitable profession for him. Concerned about Anil's higher studies, he admitted Anil to the Birla Vishvakarma Mahavidyalaya Engineering College at Vallabh Vidyanagar in Gujarat, one of the oldest and best reputed colleges in the area. He also ensured that Anil went to college at a place where there were no theatres! However, this did not deter the young film buff, as he discovered that the college was actually situated between two cities, Ahmedabad and Baroda, and both had many theatres. Anil watched 105 movies in the first year itself! Possibly, these movies contributed towards building an emotional self for the young man who was patriotic at heart and empathetic to the needs of others. It was a time in India where optimism and nationalism were in the air. Anil's deep-rooted nationalist feelings might have taken root in this period.

Anil's leadership qualities further strengthened at the engineering college. Although, always courageous, he became gutsy during these years. He narrated an episode from the time when college elections were being held. In a reflective mood, Naik stated, 'The local leader approached me and told me to withdraw my candidature for the post of General Secretary. I looked him in the eye and replied that I was not sure of even contesting the election but now that you are threatening me, I have made up my mind. I will certainly contest the election.' He not only contested the election but also won it.

Anil worked hard and passed his engineering exam with flying colours. He graduated with a bachelor's degree in mechanical engineering. Having completed his education and keen on participating in nation-building, Anil wished to be part of companies like L&T, Voltas or Tatas. L&T was his dream company when in 1964 he moved to Bombay, the commercial capital of India, in search of a job.

Chapter 3

Journey from a Village to the World

*It is good to have an end to the journey,
but what matters at the end is the journey.*

—Ernest Hemingway

The history of every growing and modernizing economy is one of urbanization. When village folks migrate to cities, they must adapt to a whole new way of life, and more often than not, the 'charmed village ways' are lost forever. In this transition, society changes as a whole but the individual represents change at the atomic level. Young Naik went through this journey early in life. How did the village boy cope with the world of work? How did he adjust to city life? Did he get cowed down by the pressures of city life or establish himself on his own terms? It is an interesting piece of Naik's story that takes into account his journey from the village to the outside world, from boyhood to being the promising business manager at L&T, who eventually led and shaped the company.

Armed with his engineering degree and a note of recommendation from his father, Anil first went to Viren J. Shah, MD of Mukand Iron & Steel Works Ltd for a job. He had made several mistakes in his application form and was rejected due to his lack of proficiency in English. The personnel manager advised him to improve his English-language skills. It was Anil's first realization of his inadequacy in written and spoken English. He made a mental note and decided to work on it.

FIRST JOB IN BOMBAY

Although Naik wanted to join L&T, he could not do so right away as L&T was known to recruit students only from the prestigious Indian Institutes of Technology (IIT)[14] and Victoria Jubilee Technology Institute (VJTI)[15]. Hence, Anil found employment at an engineering firm called Nestor Boilers as workshop supervisor. He did well, and his Parsi bosses were happy with him. However, there was a change of management and ownership at Nestor Boilers within a year as the owners had to sell the company. A father-son duo from East Africa bought the company—the father was about 60 and the son around 35 years old. The work environment at Nestor Boilers changed with the change in leadership. The earlier Parsis were known to be gentle and humane but that was not true of

---

[14]Indian Institute of Technology (IIT) is one of the most respected among the engineering institutions in India.
[15]Victoria Jubilee Technology Institute (VJTI) has been one of the respected among engineering institutes in Mumbai. The name of this institute was later changed to Veermata Jijabai Technology Institute.

the new owners. The son was rough with the workers and employees. As a result, within three months all the senior staff left. Naik was loaded with more and more responsibility. At the age of 23, he became workshop-in-charge with all technical responsibilities.

While the work responsibilities did not bother him, Naik was concerned about how discourteously the boss behaved with the staff and his unpleasant attitude in general. Once he overheard the son speaking rudely with Poonawala, a quality control person, drawing a salary of ₹750 a month. He said, 'I can get this job done in ₹250. Why should I pay you ₹750?' Naik felt that his boss was crossing boundaries. That is when he asked himself, 'Would my father agree to tolerate this?' He got the answer from within, 'No.'

In that moment, he made up his mind to leave the job. The human relations practice of the new boss triggered this decision. It is an interesting reflection that talent joins companies, but professionals leave bosses! That is always the reality. It was perhaps this reality for young Naik that helped him understand the importance of human relations in management. Frustrated with Nestor Boilers, Naik reasoned with himself, 'What is the point of working in a company where people are not valued?' He therefore started to apply to engineering companies for an alternative job. Naik recalls, 'I worked hard and was the darling of the owners. Naturally then, they would not let me go. Ultimately, they did not give me the "leave salary". Yet, I left.'

Naik was thrilled to see a newspaper advertisement announcing openings at his dream company, L&T. He applied and was called for the interview. Though he was not from one of the IITs, his experience at Nestor Boilers helped him get this interview call.

Tim Baker, works manager at L&T, interviewed him and found him suitable for the job. He was offered the post of assistant engineer at a salary of ₹760. In the next round of interviews, a stern man who was Baker's boss, Gunnar Hansen grilled the young engineer. Among the tough questions, he casually asked this— 'How many people report to you?' Naik answered, '350 people.' Hansen remarked, '350 people is a lot and you will not be getting that kind of opportunity and responsibility at L&T for a long time.' Unfamiliar with the norms of communication in English, Naik literally translated his thought from Gujarati to English and responded, 'Who knows? Time will tell.' Hansen took offence and considered this reply rather impudent and a sign of overconfidence. He instructed Baker to downgrade the post offered to Naik to junior engineer at a salary of ₹670. Naik was downgraded in salary, grade and cadre—all within a matter of half an hour. Baker was apologetic, but Naik comforted him and simply said it was his dream to join L&T.

METEORIC RISE IN THE DREAM COMPANY

Naik joined L&T as junior engineer in 1965, with two obvious disadvantages: he was from a non-IIT background and was not proficient in English. However, this boy from a village in Gujarat was fearless. When he entered L&T's premises on the first day, the overwhelming feeling was that of realizing his dream.

Naik's attitude to work was deeply influenced by

the Bhagavad Gita. The following verse was especially meaningful to him.

कर्मण्येवाधिकारस्ते माफलेषुकदाचन।
माकर्मफलहेतुर्भूर्मा ते सङ्गोस्त्वकर्मणि॥

Meaning,

'You have every right to work but not to expect the fruits of it. Therefore, let the focus be on work and not on the fruits.'

Naik, raised on the values of 'work is worship', calls himself a *Karmayogi*[16]. He inherited the idea that there is no substitute for hard work. He followed his own standards that far exceeded the norms of work at L&T. He would take responsibility voluntarily. He would reach office before anyone else. He stayed back after everyone left, even though nobody was looking over his shoulder. He would put in about 16 hours of work a day. 'I used to work 100 hours a week, which is twice the required number of hours,' he said in an SPJIMR researcher interview. 'In my 54 years at L&T, I must have put 108 years of effort for the company,' he added with a smile. When asked, 'How and when do you relax?' he answered with a smile, 'When I am working.'

Naik's working style was different; he would try to innovate to be more efficient. The managers at L&T had set certain processes for smooth operations. The practice at the time for inter-departmental communication was to put papers in the out-tray that the peon would pick up and deliver

---

[16]*Karmayogi* is spiritual path in Hinduism based on the 'yoga of action'. To a karma yogi, work done well is a form of prayer.

to the mail room. Another peon would then despatch and distribute these to the addressees. This pick-up and despatch involving two peons would happen once or twice a day. This process meant that often the paper would be delivered the next day. For Naik, it meant a day wasted before his paper reached the foreman. In addition to this, Naik would worry whether the written communication was fully understood as intended.

He therefore changed the process. He would simply walk down to the foreman, explain and discuss the drawings and hand them over. He would also walk to the stores and give his requirement of material to be delivered. In fact, he would even go and check whether the material had been delivered! To him, it saved precious time. He appreciated the importance of well-laid processes but not at the cost of time and efficiency. He used this insight when he became a manager to pay more attention to the processes that streamlined work. When Baker learned about this, he was happy and appreciated Naik's zeal to do the job seamlessly. Baker also remarked, 'I now understand why you are never on your seat!'

Naik worked on the shop floor along with the workers. He was at home with workers and treated everyone as his extended family. His memory was excellent and he remembered and addressed everyone by their names. As a result, he mingled well with workers and developed a strong rapport of mutual trust and friendship. His colleagues and seniors, on the other hand, warned him that it was unsafe to stay back at night as the workers were aggressive and notoriously rowdy. However, he was fearless and reposed faith in his relationship with the workers.

His bosses, especially Baker, were happy with him, and Naik rapidly rose to positions of increasing importance. Baker put him in charge of the 'Three-month Graduate Apprentice Engineers Orientation Programme' designed for new recruits. L&T recruited toppers from IIT and VJTI, fresh out of college. Naik coordinated their activities and they soon learnt the practical aspects of working on the shop floor. With his people skills, it did not take long for Naik to develop a bond of friendship with them. Together, they would resolve engineering issues and learn from each other. His rapport with them was so strong that many of them later took up leadership positions at L&T, such as K. Venkataramanan from IIT Delhi and V.K. Magapu from IIT Madras.

Naik's hard work and appreciation from the management created a positive feedback loop. He could vividly recall all the promotions in the first decade with precise dates and numbers. 'I was appointed junior engineer with a salary of ₹670. On confirmation, within six months, I was promoted as assistant engineer with a salary of ₹760. Immediately, after one year in the organization, I became workshop-in-charge with a hike in salary to ₹1,325 with 800 people reporting to me,' Naik reminisced. He chuckled, 'I had proved Hansen wrong when he said that 350 is a large number and you will not be getting that kind of opportunity and responsibility at L&T for a long time.'

In the meantime, Baker had to leave Bombay and shift to L&T's workshop in Kansbahal near Rourkela. Naik had a new boss, Mohan Pherwani. The new boss was also happy with his performance and his zeal for work. Pherwani depended on Naik for workshop load implementation and handling union workers as he found it challenging to directly handle the workers. Naik was best suited to the task of managing workers and unions. Baker had left behind a note recommending that Naik be promoted to the next level, and Pherwani did so without any hesitation, as he wanted to encourage this gutsy boy.

In Naik's words, 'It was a record in L&T when I was promoted as assistant manager with a salary of ₹1,500 within three years of joining.' He added, 'I was promoted on the fast track to the post of production manager in 1970.'

EYES WIDE OPEN TO SEE

Naik went on his first official foreign tour to Great Britain, Germany, Canada and the US in 1970. This was the first time he went abroad on L&T work and was fascinated by the entire experience. He was impressed by the infrastructure and network of roads and rail system, as well as the clusters of towering buildings in the centre of the city called downtown. Little did he know at that time that he would one day bring this experience to India!

He minutely observed the people working on the shop floor, and was impressed by the work culture and the processes. No one shouted; no one interfered in the work of another—there was a seamless flow of output. He understood the importance of laying down processes to avoid confusion and chaos. Each time Naik saw a better way of doing something, he made a mental note of it.

Naik was also amazed with the culture and professional approach of his hosts in these countries. He found that people would not beat around the bush but come straight to the point. They were polite, respectful and formal. He returned to India with several lessons from this experience and aspired to introduce the same culture in his organization. This was 1970, and Naik had not even dreamt that he would be the change agent for his organization!

Having said this, implementing new processes in a production line is easier said than done. Discipline remained a continuing problem at L&T's Powai workshop. Workers would go fishing in Powai Lake during working hours, punch the register before their shift ended at midnight and simply not listen to anyone. Naik decided to deal with these contentious issues head-on. He would make surprise visits to the workshop at midnight and stand near the attendance punching machine. The workers would not like it, but he would speak with them in a friendly manner. Thanks to his elephantine memory, he was able to recall personal details and ask them about their families and their home. The workers respected him for his care and concern, and they were willing to abide by his mandate for discipline.

Naik was further promoted to the position of deputy general manager (DGM) in 1974. Reminiscing, Naik looked at the horizon from his window and narrated with a smile of satisfaction, 'My work was rewarded as I got six promotions in nine years. I was the youngest DGM.' He distinctly remembered his early days in L&T even after 54 years. Indeed, it was a meteoric rise!

During an interview with Bloomberg Quint,[17] he said that

---

[17] The interview 'The Life and Time of L&T' is available at <https://www.youtube.com/watch?v=Qw7uQRzZA-c> (Accessed 1 Nov 2019).

he was proud to have overcome the disadvantage of being from a non-IIT background with limited proficiency in English and competed successfully with IIT graduates. He continued to put in long hours at work. Most of the time, he would be the first to enter at 7.30 a.m. and go home late at night. This routine continued for many years even as the company touched greater heights of achievement.

UNDETERRED BY SLOW GROWTH

Compared to the exciting decade of 1965–75, Naik's next decade in L&T was relatively slow. One reason could be that the business environment in India had become heavily controlled and restrictive. The government was leaning more towards socialist policies. High income tax and corporate tax coupled with the drive for nationalization had a crippling effect on businesses. The Licence Permit Raj also restricted the new entry of firms. The MRTP Act placed ceilings on capacity expansion. On the political front, Emergency was declared in 1975–77, creating an environment of fear and autocracy. L&T suffered as large business houses in India shelved their expansion plans.

The second reason could be a change in the culture of L&T. After four decades, Holck-Larsen, co-founder of L&T, stepped down as chairman after a long and eventful stint. Simultaneously, it was time for the European managers to retire. Senior Indian managers were appointed as directors based on their experience. Slowly, the system of performance-based evaluation gave way to seniority. For someone like Naik whose promotions were on a fast-track until 1974, the period of 1974–86 seemed dull, but he hung on. Many of his colleagues moved to better jobs and even went abroad. But not Naik. He was so committed to L&T that thinking of an alternative employment was out of the question. On the contrary, he was thinking of taking on larger responsibilities and a leadership position. That finally happened in 1986 when he was promoted as general manager (GM).

Sucheta Dalal of Money Life[18] once asked Naik, 'Did you get frustrated in this period? Did you have an opportunity to go elsewhere?' Naik replied, 'Yes, I did get frustrated in this period as I was used to fast-track promotions, and I was working hard.' He added, 'But I would not go anywhere. Despite having opportunities, I did not go for even one interview.' He gave his reasons, 'It may sound strange, but at L&T I got the best opportunity to exploit my skills as an engineer as well as work for the good of the country. I don't think there was any other company that could provide me that kind of a platform.'

Later, in an interview to Bloomberg Quint,[19] he said, 'I have a deep sense of passion, devotion, commitment and conviction for L&T.' He added, 'L&T provides tremendous freedom and a sense of ownership. For me, L&T is my life. I am devoted to L&T.'

So what made him tick and stick? On reflecting on this question, he opined that he really enjoyed his work, and to

---

[18] A.M. Naik's interview in Money Life. Available at <http://www.suchetadalal.com/?id=4f28061f-8177-7bb2-492e8bb5b8ad&base=sections&f&t=AM+Naik+-+A+rare+interview+to+MoneyLIFE> (Accessed on 1 Nov 2019).

[19] A.M. Naik's interview with Bloomberg Quint. Available at <https://www.youtube.com/watch?v=Qw7uQRzZA-c> (Accessed on 1 Nov 2019).

enjoy your work is a blessing. He enjoyed the freedom and feeling of ownership that L&T offered. Maybe he had stumbled on to his own mantra of how to build an institution. Perhaps these experiences seeped into his management style—to create an atmosphere of engagement in the company and enjoyment of the work for employees.

EMERGING AS AN EFFICIENT MANAGER

How did Naik learn the principles of management on the job in the first decade of his career at L&T?

Naik meticulously implemented policies. He planned the process in such a way that there would be minimum disruptions and seamless flow of output. He was quick to resolve unexpected issues so that it was not difficult to achieve targets. He was setting up processes for minimum wastage of time and resources, and followed metrics for strict quality control. He managed people well and in turn received support from his team. This was due to his relations with people that he had risen to managerial levels while working by their side. Managing and motivating the team was most important, and Naik did that well. He had the reputation of being a people's person. He was a meticulous manager, who would delegate but not leave anything to chance. He planned his schedules well and delivered on time. Typifying the behaviour enumerated in the Mindset-Behaviour-Action Grid, he practised the process of cyclical learning: Action-Observation-Benchmark-Review-Act. This means he received the feedback of his own actions through the process of observation and benchmarking along with the review that further improved the process.

It was his deep sense of commitment and belonging to L&T that took him through the dormant decade of his career to emerge as 'Nayak', the hero in the next decade, even as he exercised his Shaper skills from high up the corporate ladder.

A LEADER THINKS ABOUT THE FUTURE: CREATING CAPACITY

Taking ownership and leadership came naturally to Naik years before he reached the top position. Even when he was the DGM, at mid-level in terms of management hierarchy, he was already thinking about L&T's future path. Equipped with two decades of learning on the job, Naik was instinctively taking on the role of a Shaper. His thinking was driven by the idea: 'What should be done so that L&T enters the next orbit?' He focused his attention to the structural changes necessary to increase L&T's scale and redefine its scope. He started to shape L&T by taking steps to scale up the Heavy Engineering and Hydrocarbon Engineering divisions.

The Strategy to go Global

It was then the 1980s and globalization was the buzzword. Most companies were eager to participate as the world was coming closer and globalization was making the world a global village.[20] L&T had already succeeded at being the best in the country. The next step was to compete globally. Already, ECC, the construction division of L&T, had some

---

[20]Theodore Levitt, 'Globalization of Markets', *Harvard Business Review*, May 1983.

experience in constructing complex structures in the Middle East and Gulf countries in the 1970s and 1980s. These projects could be viewed in the category of 'sporadic exports' that help businesses to test the global market, and were the learning ground that helped ECC become more confident to handle larger and more complex projects.

However, Naik was not satisfied with these sporadic exports. He dreamt of other L&T divisions entering the global market. He wanted to create a lasting presence for L&T in the international markets with engineering equipment and projects. He started by working to change the scale of operations to enable the Heavy Engineering and Hydrocarbon Engineering divisions to enter the export market for large heavy machinery and projects that even included catering to the oil and gas sector.

Usually, businesses look for new global pastures in response to either a slow down or saturation of domestic demand. For L&T, the order book was full and the domestic demand was robust. Even then, Naik was planning for the future and going international. He thought it was a good strategy to plan now so that the organization was equipped to handle local and global demands in the future. In Naik, a Shaper of L&T was at work. What's more, he started planning this strategy in the early 1980s when India was still a closed economy. Naturally, the ride was turbulent.

When Naik and his team approached the board of directors at L&T with a proposal to set up a facility for Heavy Engineering at Hazira, it was a tough sell. In the 1980s, the board needed much persuasion to approve the Hazira project. Naik was still a DGM, and he had to present to the board the rationale of investment on the one hand and the execution plan on the other. He was persuading the board to approve a budget of ₹38 crore.

The project was a big risk by L&T standards at that time. The board had several questions. Have you assessed the risk? What if it does not work out? Who takes responsibility? Naik responded, 'We have assessed risk, and we will mitigate it. I take the responsibility and we will make it work.' What was on display here were the qualities of entrepreneurship and risk-taking, and willingness to take responsibility at the level of a manager. Who could predict at that time that this person would become the leader and the Shaper of the organization and bring in a transformation? The board finally approved, though with some reservations.

Venkataramanan, who worked alongside Naik for five decades, and was the former CEO and MD of L&T said, 'This was Naik's vision—L&T was quite small at that time. He was thinking of achieving a scale in terms of size that world-class equipment would require, maybe five to ten times larger than what we were producing at Powai.'[21] The setup of a new manufacturing facility on the coast was required because exports for large equipment that needed to be shipped could not be done from the landlocked Powai. The entire exercise revolved around the Orbit Changing Policies.

Selecting the Location

Naik had assembled a team of engineers for the project, who went through an exercise to shortlist a suitable coastal location

---

[21]Merchant, *The Nationalist*.

somewhere in Kerala, Karnataka, Maharashtra or Gujarat. They were keen on a location that opened to the Arabian Sea and connected to the Western world. The team discussed threadbare the pros and cons of each location, in terms of availability of infrastructure, the culture of the workers, and the policies and philosophy of the state government towards industrialization. The team thus zeroed in on Hazira in Gujarat, located virtually on the shore of the Arabian Sea.

Hazira was then emerging as an important hub of mega-development. Large corporates such as ONGC, Reliance and Essar were also planning their projects in the same region. Krishak Bharati Cooperative Limited (KRIBHCO) was already there. Hazira was also close to Ubharat near Surat which was the gas landfall point for Bombay High. The Hazira–Vijaipur–Jagdishpur (HVJ) pipeline was to start from Hazira.

'Hazira was not some obscure and uninhabited place. It would become the most happening place shortly,' Naik said. The best part of the story was that there was plenty of land available. It was a strategic location from where it could cater to international markets. The markets of the Middle East and Gulf countries, figuratively speaking, were just a stone's throw away. But, L&T being the first to establish themselves at Hazira, had to deal with a range of teething troubles from landfill issues to struggling for a licence to begin manufacture. The first 200 acres of Hazira land was bought from the government. The land was on the waterfront as per the requirement. The land report and assessment read: 'It was a trapezoidal piece of land, next to Tapti river, touching the Arabian sea. The land had 1.6 km of waterfront and 1.8 km of road boundary.' Hazira was a marshland in 1983, so was Powai in 1948. It was the founder Holck-Larsen who created the Powai facilities out of the marshland. It was now time for the Shaper Naik to convert the Hazira marshland into a modern state-of-the-art manufacturing complex. Not an easy task by any standard.

CONSTRUCTION CHALLENGES: A MIRACLE ON MARSH

Naik described the land as if it was yesterday that he started work on the Hazira marshland: 'In high tide, the sea and river merged. One could not tell where the land ends and the river starts. All you could see was a black strip of road. If you keep walking, you will fall into the river. Only if you go during the low tide, you can see the river and the marshy land. We would walk with gumboots along the entire stretch of the land and finally chose a spot with the best navigation characteristics—1.6 km of waterfront.' This was followed by a navigation study to understand the depth of the river. 'We also found that five feet of earth needed to be filled up as there was significant difference between high tide and low tide,' he added. The excitement of the new adventure that the team undertook more than three decades ago is visible even today in Naik's narration.

Venkataramanan went to Hazira as a project manager in 1984. He had a strong background in R&D and played a significant role in sorting out the initial challenges of construction that required piling—a construction method for laying a deep foundation. As the entire area was a marshland, there was no rock upon which the piles could be built. Venkataramanan had to study in detail about piles and learn about pre-cast and pre-stressed concrete though his specialization was chemical engineering.

Naik would visit every week and was fully involved in all processes from the selection of workers and staff to planning and guiding the construction of the manufacturing facility. Venkataramanan recalls those heady and exciting days: 'We had to build the structure at Hazira on concrete column piles. The work schedules were tight and needed constant monitoring. Naik travelled to Hazira every week when there was weekly off at Powai, and I travelled to Mumbai when there was weekly off at Hazira. Both of us did not take a weekly off for about three years!'

Naik was a hard taskmaster. But he would not tell others to do anything that he did not do himself. As Venkataramanan recalled, 'Naik would work with us. At times, it got tiring, but we could pull through as our leader would always be there to keep our spirits high.' What Naik did here was to energize his people to internalize the organizational mission and values. Often Shapers impart relevant values through personal relationships.

The construction at Hazira was a complex project that also demanded the best use of Naik's people skills. For instance, while the construction was still underway, the team at Hazira faced a new challenge. They were sourcing coarse panna sand for the project from the nearby villages of Mora and Damka. Despite having permission from the collector and taluka chief, the villagers protested and eight to ten women lay down in front of the trucks, thereby stopping movement. The team had no clue how to resolve this kind of crisis. Naik plunged into action. He went to the villages and spoke persuasively with the protestors in their own language. They listened as he not only spoke to them in Gujarati, but also in the dialect of that region, Surti. Naik sincerely explained to them that this complex would create new jobs, bring roads, power, sanitation and above all, prosperity to the region. He assured them that the company was engaged in the very last phase of earth filling and not an inch more would be filled. He spoke to the people with great empathy as if they were his extended family. It was Naik's people skills at work that rescued the project from this imbroglio.

Even as the workshop was taking shape and the starting of the manufacturing facility was about two years away, Naik, the quintessential Shaper looked into the future to resolve the next big question: How to get skilled workers? He made a master plan to source and train people. L&T established a training centre in Udhna, a town about 30 km away from Hazira. It recruited students from 500 schools in Gujarat by setting up a process that attracted the best students. Even as the Hazira facility was being readied, the team started a small workshop where the trainees from Udhna could work on small engineering jobs, getting ready for the bigger jobs. Two projects were on-going simultaneously: first the hardscape—creating capacity by way of a massive fabrication yard and installing machinery and equipment; and second, the softscape—training manpower.

Naik also had an eye for finding the right people for the job and the persuasion skills to convince them to take it up. Naik had thought of V.K. Magapu who was earlier with L&T but had left the company to move to Canada. During one of his trips to the US, Naik specially went to New Brunswick in Canada to meet Magapu to persuade him to re-join L&T. He had an overnight conversation with Magapu and his wife Lakshmi that started at 9.00 p.m. and ended the next day in the wee hours of the morning at six! Naik convinced Magapu to be in-charge at Hazira in 1987 when the project was almost at its finishing stage. Naik left Magapu's residence at 7.00 a.m. only after he had accomplished the mission.

Eventually, Magapu returned to India, joined L&T and went to Hazira. Still fresh in his memory, he narrated an anecdote about their experience with the L&T Board. He remembered all the numbers as he said: 'We were the bad boys of the boardroom. We were overshooting the budget by ₹12 crore. We explained to the board that this happened due to land restoration, piling and girder rejoining. Eventually, the board was satisfied when everyone saw and agreed that Hazira was a miracle built on marsh.'

It took 30 months to ready the Hazira complex. The transformation of Hazira from a swamp into a manufacturing complex that builds equipment for nuclear-powered submarines, nuclear reactors, fast interceptor vessels, and offshore oil and gas platforms is one of the most extraordinary stories in Indian corporate history. 'We started Phase I with 200 acres. Subsequently, over the years, 555 acres were added to house more facilities. The complex finally measures 755 acres of land of which 555 acres are used for various manufacturing facilities whereas the remaining land is used for defence, which includes the Armoured Systems Complex that was inaugurated by Prime Minister Narendra Modi in 2019,' Naik said with a smile of satisfaction.

These efforts led to L&T assuming a leadership position in the design, development and manufacture of missiles and weapon systems. Indigenizing the manufacture of critical equipment for the defence sector and process industries was an operation L&T had kick-started decades ago. The company also forged a vibrant relationship with national and international bodies for defence research and development. One such defence collaboration was also with Russia.

Today, Hazira's Modular Fabrication Facility (MFF), is counted among the best in the world, with a 50,000 ton annual capacity. The MFF designs critical equipment for the upstream cluster of the hydrocarbon spectrum not just for India but overseas too. L&T has created much of the Hazira skyline, by designing and executing all the towers and columns of the Reliance Petrochemical complex. Hazira currently employs 2,000 engineers and technologists. The campus has 12,000 to 16,000 people, working on local and global projects.

L&T also had a shipyard capable of constructing vessels up to 150-metre-long and displacing of 20,000 tons at its heavy engineering complex at Hazira. The shipyard constructed specialized heavy-lift ships, CNG carriers, chemical tankers, defence and para-military vessels, submarines and other role-specific vessels. When L&T was doing 100–200 ton jobs in the 1980s, Naik was planning to expand the scale 10 times. When L&T built more facilities in other locations of the country, some rationalization of product portfolio took place. Hazira was exclusive to heavy engineering projects and the shipyard was shifted to Kattapulli in Tamil Nadu to enable economies of scale.

Even while engaging in core engineering projects, Naik

did not lose sight of the smaller details. He was passionate about landscaping. As R.N. Mukhija, former director and board member of L&T remarked, 'He would not allow any facility to start unless landscaping was complete. Every inch of the land had to be treated, either green or paved.' The green cover also helped to create a dust-free environment.

The realization of the Hazira dream brought out the leadership qualities in Naik. He emerged as a thought leader who followed an integrated model of leadership.

ACTION GRID FOR A LEADER

Policies	• Capacity creation to be future ready • Focus on long-term policies
Processes	• Handle short-run issues but simultaneously work on long-run goals • Demonstrate single-minded commitment once a decision is made • Identify the obstacles and seek the best way to deal with it—break it, go around it or navigate it • Insist on a systems approach of cyclical learning
People	• Understand the customer and community perspective • Influence people with motivation and engagement
Performance	• Develop an integrated model of leadership

We believe that Naik ticked all the boxes in the Action Grid for Leaders. Institutional leaders do three things consistently: first, they plan with vision and values; second, they organize with alignment and clarity; and third, they control with motivation and involvement. In this way, they amalgamate and synergize managing, directing and engaging, that not only serves as an integrated model but helps shape and expedite their movement into becoming future transformers.[22]

Naik's ascent in L&T gathered pace. When the Hazira project was under construction, the management recognized his hard work. He was promoted to the position of GM in 1986. With the completion of Hazira, the then chairman of L&T, N.M. Desai realized Naik's enormous entrepreneurial ability. He said, 'L&T would not have been where it is today if Naik was not there.' He was inducted as a member of the board in 1989.

---

[22] Jim Fisher, *The Thoughtful Leader: A Model of Integrative Leadership* (Rotman-UTP Publishing, Rotman School of Management, 2016).

Chapter 4

L&T Adapts to Its DNA

> Aligning to one's DNA is similar to finding your Atma, core of yourself.
>
> —Anonymous

We asked Naik, chairman of L&T, 'What is the most significant contribution you made in your long memorable career of 54 years at L&T?' Without batting an eyelid, he answered, 'The demerger of the cement business and the transfer of equity shares to the L&T Employees Welfare Trust, remain my most important contribution.' He added with a smile, 'I helped L&T adapt to its DNA.'

What could he have meant by this statement?

Corporate DNA is a metaphorical term, based on the meaning of DNA in biology. In life sciences, it is DNA that carries the code of genetic instructions which make living organisms. The equivalent for a corporation, corporate DNA for short, is defined as the 'visions, values, and a sense of purpose that bind an organization together. It is that which enables individuals to understand and absorb the mission and challenge of the whole enterprise.'

When we speak about organizational culture being transmitted to generations of employees, it is akin to the institution's encoded DNA being transmitted. Organizational culture influences the perception of a company in the eyes of the people, whether they are consumers or employees. For instance, the culture of Tata is associated with 'trust' and Google with 'innovation.' To almost every well-known company we can assign such a character. It is well recognized that corporate culture has a significant impact on organizational health and performance. A strong positive culture is a true asset. Such an asset is not in the strict economic sense but the emotional sense. The DNA of the company is established 'during its initial stages' reflecting the 'personal and professional values' of the founders.

L&T is a company that has created a strong sense of emotional bonding for employees over several decades. This valuable equity of emotional ownership (as distinct from financial ownership) does not appear as a balance sheet item. But, it does have value, and it is this value that Naik desired to retain forever. How Naik helped L&T to realign to its corporate DNA is elucidated through a backstory provided in the next section.

THE BACKSTORY: TRYST WITH A TAKEOVER

It was the late 1980s. The Indian corporate sector was assailed by a spate of corporate takeover attempts by two Dubai-based siblings—Manu and Kishore Chhabria. Manu

Chhabria, a debonair non-resident Indian (NRI), had made a fortune in Dubai through his electronics trading activity. Loaded with bags of money, Manu could plough into the Indian corporate market quite intrusively. He already had to his credit a series of high-profile buys of listed companies such as Shaw Wallace, Dunlop and Hindustan Dorr-Oliver. Subsequently, Manu Chhabria set his lustful eyes on L&T by cornering shares from the secondary market. The red light of danger started blinking in L&T's boardroom. The then chairman of L&T, Narottam Desai, needed a saviour, a white knight with deep pockets and a commercial reason to save L&T from a potential predator.

L&T's chairman sought out Dhirubhai Ambani, chairman of Reliance Industries Ltd (RIL) as a white knight and requested him to invest in the company as a counter against Chhabria.[23] In takeover jargon, a white knight is a friendly acquirer who acquires a corporation to avoid it from being taken over by an unfriendly acquirer. Although the target company does not remain independent, acquisition by a white knight is still preferred to a hostile takeover. RIL was a major corporation and growing dramatically while Ambani, who embodied a rags-to-riches story, was widely perceived as a daring and imaginative entrepreneur. L&T had a long-standing business relationship with RIL, as it had executed construction and fabrication of several projects for RIL. Through this business association, RIL had developed an appreciation for L&T's engineering skills and thus agreed to act as a white knight to thwart the Chhabria threat. RIL immediately bought a sizable

---

[23]Merchant, *The Nationalist*, p.96.

chunk of shares of L&T from the open market and continued to corner more shares. Within two years, RIL had increased its stake to 18.5 per cent by spending close to ₹190 crore. Armed with this sizeable stake, RIL sought and was granted, three seats on the L&T Board.

However, RIL could not take over the company. Indian public financial institutions and major shareholders of L&T were resistant to a change of management control at India's top engineering company. Thanks to the resistance of these institutions, RIL had to be content with being a passive investor on the board of L&T. This situation continued for 14 years, a long period for a high-growth company to lock up its money passively in shares.

In November 2001, RIL decided to sell its stake to another eponymous business group, Aditya Birla Group (ABG), headed by the young and dashing Kumar Mangalam Birla. Once again, alarm bells rang at L&T. The board became apprehensive about the disruptive and unproductive side-effects of a hostile takeover.

In the meantime, Naik had risen to the top leadership position of CEO and MD at L&T in 1999. He had so strongly absorbed the ethos of the company during his long career at L&T that his life entirely revolved around L&T and its functioning. L&T was his life, and he felt that there was no life without an independent L&T. When the exchange of the L&T shares took place between RIL and ABG, Naik had been in the top job for two years. It was certainly not the time when he would have welcomed an existential crisis for the company. However, it was not a matter that he could time. He found the body and the soul of L&T squeezed between two of the largest corporate groups in India, RIL and ABG.

Emotional Ownership

Naik very well knew the dictum, 'If a company is cheap and does not have a single owner with a large shareholding, it becomes an easy takeover target.' L&T suffered from both conditions. First, L&T shares were cheap, despite being engaged in complex high-value engineering marvels and infrastructure projects in India and abroad. Its low market value made it an attractive takeover target. Secondly, there was no possessive parent watching L&T like a darling ward. There was no active promoter who was involved in its management. As stated earlier, L&T had been successful because of its employees, who did not own the company's equity, but behaved possessively as though they owned the company.

Naik and his team understood that mergers, acquisitions and takeovers are part of the reality in the competitive world of business. Faced with one, it is easy for companies to play the victim card as takeover threats generate a lot of heat, occupy a lot of mind space and are extremely distracting due to media coverage. However, it was not the way out.

To get the situation back on track, Naik did some serious soul-searching, both for himself and the company. He had to think and rethink the true purpose of L&T and why it existed as well as his position viz-à-viz the company and what role he should play in advancing L&T's mission. Although he was on the hot seat, Naik was clear on one thing—the life and existence of L&T was at stake, and that was more important than anything else. Naik experienced the need for great mindfulness and deep reflection almost to the level of meditation. He asked simple existential questions: Who owns L&T? How has it arrived at the level it is today? What is the DNA of L&T?

It suddenly hit him like a bolt from the blue that L&T was emotionally owned by workers though they were not its financial owners. L&T's culture had been transmitted from one generation of employees to another, all the while preserving the company's DNA. It was the employees, who were the real owners of the company; they held 'emotional equity,' thus creating a strong positive culture in the company. This soft asset of emotional equity was not valued in the balance sheet, but it certainly made L&T what it was. In companies, as with individuals, existential threats awaken simple truths. What was on display was the Shaper who did not just find a fork in the historical road: he helped to create it. This fork in the road by way of emotional equity was a new concept that had never been considered in the accounting and valuing of companies so far.

Although figuratively, Naik and his colleagues arrived at a clear distinction between two types of equities—financial and emotional—they argued that the investors were owners of the financial, whereas workers were owners of the emotional equity. Very likely, the roots of this line of thinking would have sprung from a high level of emotional intelligence and empathy with the employees. The team advanced the thought process, brainstormed and concluded that it was the workers that had nurtured the company and therefore, emotional equity too should receive an appropriate status, just as financial equity. They raised two questions: How could the value of this emotional equity be assessed? How could this emotional ownership be aligned so that L&T could live long?

Naik and his team then looked for answers within the company and reviewed L&T's strategy. For years, L&T had chosen to remain in the area of producing machines which would manufacture goods. It was a strategic decision to produce only capital goods and not consumer goods. However, it had so happened that as part of the company's vertical integration, it had entered into the cement business. But cement manufacture was neither profitable nor quite aligned with the company's strategy of being only in the capital goods sector. For some years, the company had been toying with the idea of hiving off its cement business. The team realized during discussions with ABG that the Birla Group was mainly interested in L&T's cement business.

Naik wondered whether Birla would buy only the cement manufacturing business. If ABG would agree, then it could save the rest of L&T. An L&T Employees Welfare Trust could be created and ABG could transfer its shares to the trust against the cement business of L&T. Such a shareholding pattern would serve a dual purpose: first, it could ring-fence L&T from future corporate raiders as the employees would have substantial voting rights and second, it would further strengthen the employees' sense of belonging. The team was satisfied as a good solution had emerged to protect L&T from any takeover attempts in the future. Naik and his team in the top management were convinced about this remedy to save L&T.

WORKERS BECOME OWNERS

To execute the idea, Naik and his management team needed to implement a four-step action plan:

1. They first needed to demerge the cement business from L&T and negotiate with ABG only for the cement business.
2. Being a hard-core engineer, he needed to be aware about the company's finances and valuation of its cement business. Naik thus consulted financial experts and investment bankers to get their perspective about the financials. He also approached financial institutions to earn their confidence.
3. The entire deal had to be within the boundaries of the Company Law and other securities norms. For this, he reached out to the government, experts in the field and built a network of contacts.
4. Naik needed to convince his employees and reassure them that he was not selling them cheap. He needed to communicate to them to get their buy-in. Naik addressed several meetings where he said, 'Why should we remain servants? Let us become the owners of this company.' He suggested, 'If we convert this risk into a security ring by becoming the shareholders of the company, no one can touch us.'

In 2003, after months of confidential negotiations with ABG, a deal was struck. It was spelled out in these words: 'ABG should exit L&T by selling its stake to L&T Employees Welfare Trust, and in return, ABG would receive L&T's cement business.' It was a win-win deal for both. ABG got what they wanted—the cement manufacturing business of L&T that would in turn consolidate ABG's position in the cement industry, and L&T could avoid the takeover by ABG and remain a professionally managed company.

'When L&T's history is written and rewritten, nobody will ever forget that L&T existed because of Naik,' Kumar Mangalam Birla stated while closing the deal. 'This act of empowering the employees shall go down in the corporate history of India,' he added.

The cement demerger increased the value of L&T. This kind of restructuring was uncommon in Indian capital markets at that time. It transformed L&T into a different kind of organization. Hiving off the cement division lowered the burden of debt on L&T's balance sheet. The debt–equity ratio drastically reduced from 1:1 to 0.2:1. L&T's Economic Value Add (EVA), an important indicator of the financial health of the company, swung from negative to positive. This correction in market value compelled rating analysts to take a positive view of the demerger and they changed L&T's ratings from AA+ to AAA.

Within a short period of five years, the demerger of the cement business in 2003 pushed up the market capitalization and the shareholder's value by nearly 20 times, from ₹4,592 crore in 2003 to ₹88,423 crore in 2008. In the same period, the Sensex rose by about five times from 3,153 in 2003 to 16,371 in 2008. L&T created history in re-rating of its value as the company outperformed the market by a factor of 4X. Shareholders loved Naik as the Compound Average Growth Rate (CAGR) of L&T's market capitalization for the period

2003-08 was 81 per cent against a CAGR of 39 per cent for Sensex. Such improvement in financial performance goes a long way in establishing the company in the local and global space. The company was being perceived in a new light, a fresh perspective that improved its sustainability.

CEO IS CUSTOMER-EMPLOYEE-OWNER

Naik was happy that his position of CEO worked as an acronym that also described him as Customer-Employee-Owner. At L&T, customers had always been the reason for their existence. By making Employees into Owners, the dynamics in the company changed. Naik was happy that with the cement demerger, both conditions that made the company an attractive takeover target could be resolved. One, the Employees Trust with a 12.5 per cent stake would be able to ring-fence and vote out any takeover threat. Two, the rise in the share price of L&T had created a second ring-fence ensuring that the company was not cheap anymore. Clearly, Naik's mindset was to 'Break Barriers.' He steered through obstacles and sought the best way to deal with the situation and navigate the company out of it. We refer to this ability to deal with complex situations and help an entire team to navigate ahead as 'Breaking Barriers' in the Mindset-Behaviour-Action Grid.

Chapter 5 chronicles the role Naik played in the evolution and transformation of L&T by describing the steps he took to align the organization to value creation making L&T an investor's delight.

Chapter 5

Power of Transformation

> An organization's ability to learn,
> and translate that learning into action rapidly,
> is the ultimate competitive advantage.
>
> —Jack Welch

When Naik was appointed CEO of L&T in 1999, he had a fair idea about what he needed to do with urgency. He had mentally taken on the role of a leader long before he actually stepped into the leadership role. Naik was a thought leader. He did not hesitate to introduce bold new concepts into the organization's lexicon. He announced Project Blue Chip within the first hundred days of taking on the leadership role. The project aimed to convert L&T into a blue chip company.

PROJECT BLUE CHIP

The term 'blue chip' is used in capital markets for companies whose share price gives consistently higher returns to the investors. The share price outperforms the average gain, represented by the Sensex or Nifty indices. The investors would get higher returns when the share price of L&T would rise. Naik often wondered that even though L&T was doing great work and was respected as being among the best companies in the country, its stock was not at par with its work and reputation. The returns that the investors got from investing in L&T shares were lower than what could be earned by investing in shares of companies like Reliance Industries Ltd or Hindustan Lever or Aditya Birla Group, which were considered the blue chip companies. It was a discomforting realization for him that there was something amiss.

He wondered, how do you raise the share price of your company? The share price is an outcome; so what can a company do to raise its share price? International consultancy firm BCG was appointed to look into the matter and help L&T develop the strategy. After an in-depth inquiry and discussing the issue threadbare, the engineer in Naik, who was an expert at planning schedules backward to meet a deadline, decided to start his inquiry backward on this subject. What factors determine the price of a company's share?

He studied the theories that explained this question. First, he came across the behavioural theory of stock price determination that is based on the interplay of demand and supply of shares. The daily share price is determined by how many people are willing to buy the shares and how many people are willing to sell the shares. Sentiment governs people's willingness to buy or sell, and this is, in turn, influenced by a large number of socio-politico-economic events. Share prices would rise if sentiments of optimism are higher than that of pessimism and vice versa. The behavioural theory explains the movement in the share price in the short run, perhaps on a daily, hourly, or even minute-by-minute basis.

However, it was the second, fundamental theory of stock price determination[24] that appealed to Naik. It stated that over the long run, share prices are determined by fundamental factors of the business. It further states that over the long term, share price reflects the true value of a company. The true value of a share is determined by the growth of the business as well as its profitability and return on the capital employed. When the value of the share grows, price rise would follow. The fundamental theory of stock prices was no rocket science. It did not take time for the Gujarati in Naik to comprehend the basics of *dhandho* (business).

After understanding the nitty-gritty of share price determination, Naik took a macro approach to initiate transformation in the organization. He decided to revisit L&T's vision statement to evolve a new strategy that recognized the importance of value creation. He involved a large number of people to develop the new strategy, so that there was 'buy in' for the project and resistance to change was minimal. There were four distinct ideas that emerged in the new vision statement for value creation: (*i*) enhance shareholder value; (*ii*) constantly create value; (*iii*) make L&T an Indian MNC; and (*iv*) attain global benchmarking.

---

[24]Robert G. Hagstrom, *The Warren Buffett Way* (Wiley, 1997).

Project Blue Chip articulated the concept of value creation with clarity and vigour. The team systematically worked to transform L&T into a blue chip company by creating value for its shareholders. Next, it was important for every employee of the company, especially his fellow engineer colleagues, to understand how shares are priced without involving them in fancy financial gobbledygook.

With the help of consultants, a manual of simple steps to increase the share price of L&T was created. This included: (*i*) raising the income or the top-line by taking on mega projects and growing the business; (*ii*) managing resources for efficient cost control without time or budget overruns that cause cost escalation; (*iii*) keeping track of net profit or bottom line as well as profit margin when the company was expanding, (*iv*) achieving expansion without equity dilution that would lead to a rise in net profit, resulting in the rise of Earnings Per Share (EPS); (*v*) and commanding a higher discount through the improved perception of L&T among the investing community. A sustained improvement in profitability helps to build trust, which would result in the higher price-earnings multiple (P/E) that blue chip companies command.

Though L&T was doing a great job, its profitability was low. The margin of profit in the large complex equipment that L&T manufactured was low, and the perceived risk was high. Investors did not understand the complex equipment that L&T made and therefore were not willing to give higher P/E. Naik invited capital market experts such as Anand Rathi and P.S. Subramanian of UTI to get his team to understand the relationship between L&T operations and share price. The team recognized the problem with L&T. 'It is necessary to do good work for your customers, but that is not sufficient to take care of investors. The mission was clear: Along with customer delight, create investor delight.' The share price is an outcome; it would emerge from higher profits. The path was to scale up the capacity and expand the business to garner higher profits. Going global and evolving L&T into an Indian MNC emerged as the offshoots of the strategy.

CREATING VALUE FOR STAKEHOLDERS

Engaging in businesses that create value emerged as a major plank on which Project Blue Chip rested. Historically, L&T did not make high profits and that was nothing to be ashamed of. The way of life in the 1970s and 1980s in India may seem absurd today. 'Business' and 'profit' were dirty words in socialist India. L&T was a conservative company committed to national development and not vigilant about its profitability. It was not in the DNA of L&T to be business savvy. The results of an in-house survey of top L&T employees revealed this culture. It was found that 'Top employees at L&T thought they built monuments; none of them thought that they built shareholder value.' The internal and external branding of L&T was such that no one thought they were in business. They took pride in building the tallest tower, a state-of-the-art airport and working with national institutions such as ISRO and BARC.

L&T could afford to have this stance as long as India was a closed economy. But, liberalization through the economic reforms of 1991 had opened the doors to global competition.

L&T had to compete with global companies not only in the world but also in India. It was imperative that L&T changed its strategy and became competitive by benchmarking with the best in the world.

Venkataramanan, a veteran at L&T for five decades, and CEO and MD for the period 2012–2015, said, 'Naik should be given credit for bringing a business-oriented culture into the company.' Naik was the thought leader who introduced and articulated the concept of 'value creation', which was inserted into the organization's vocabulary. It marked a radical departure from the prevailing culture in L&T. It became a prism through which every aspect of the company was viewed. 'Is it creating value?' became the new question to be asked, the standard by which every process would be measured. Value creation turned into a tool for the transformation of the organization, from the corporate level to the task level. For the first time, executives thought before taking up a project. They considered whether it was worthwhile or not to do the project. Thus, the leadership at L&T started thinking in terms of value creation, targeting turnover and profit.

S.N. Subrahmanyan (SNS), current CEO and MD at L&T said, 'It was natural for leaders of L&T divisions to take all kinds of orders to grow. But to improve the quality of work, it was important to be selective.' The internal analysis suggested that the smaller projects were a drain on the resources. A policy with some objective criteria was evolved. 'We started putting filters—on geography, on values, and on contracts,' he added. The filters changed the way projects were taken up, choosing big and more profitable projects while letting go of the smaller ones. A better risk management system was also built around the filters.

K. Venkataramanan reviewed L&T's business orientation over time. 'Today's L&T is because we could move from simple fabrication to nuclear, space, defence, oil and gas. Our construction wing moved from simple road construction to complex construction projects like airports and metros.' He pointed out that there is a need to continuously realign the strategy. 'At this stage, doing great projects is satisfying. But the profit margin in these sectors after so much of hard work is lower than in manufacturing and services. We have reached the zenith, doing more of the same. The L&T team saw the need to change track. That is how, when you see Infosys and HDFC Bank, what you see is higher profitability and market value. Currently, IT and finance are known to be the racy sectors. That is the reason we spun off Infotech and Technology Services.'

Venkataramanan also spoke about L&T's present strategy: 'In the parent L&T, there has been organic growth, but in the new area, we are trying to grow inorganically. This is the rationale to acquire Mindtree. Today, we are building tomorrow's L&T where knowledge businesses, Information Technology (IT), Internet of Things (IoT), Machine Learning have to be big. We cannot wait for another 20 years to grow.'

This readiness to shift the business focus reveals the distinction between business leaders and Shapers. It becomes apparent when one compares the way they respond to the challenge of the future. Leaders identify relevant megatrends and implicit value drivers. They exploit the existing industry structure and ensure leadership. A Shaper on the other hand is able to anticipate emerging trends and future value drivers. Naik has demonstrated the ability to anticipate the likely course of events that enabled him to decipher patterns well before they became megatrends. He re-moulded businesses accordingly. As Magapu stated: 'What Naik did in his leadership role [is that] he transformed the company from a sedate, gentlemanly company to an agile and fighting fit, competitive company. His intervention led to course correction and brought in better focus in the organization.'

It was the right time as the capital market in India had become active since the reforms of 1991. Investor expectations ran high. Business news, TV channels and a large community of equity analysts were minutely observing every move of Corporate India. Corporate communication to the media, Securities and Exchange Board of India (SEBI) and stock exchanges on yearly and quarterly basis had to be crisp and transparent. As Naik put it, 'L&T had to adapt to the new culture and perform.' The company was transforming from a 'bulky diversified conglomerate to shareholder-value driven.' The dream of 'turning L&T into an Indian MNC and world-class business conglomerate' was evolved. The 'business orientation' and 'engaging in business that creates value' was derived from the simple deductive logic of the fundamental stock market theory.

MARKET PERFORMANCE AND INVESTOR DELIGHT

Internationally, the CEOs who have created value for shareholders are celebrated with great fanfare. Jack Welch

(CEO of GE 1981–2000), Percy Barnevik (CEO of ABB 1988–96) and Larry Bossidi (CEO AlliedSignal Inc./Honeywell International Inc. 1991–2002) have all received accolades for positively impacting the company's bottom line by an X factor under their leadership. However, it can be seen that L&T stock[25] clearly outperformed GE stock and Sensex[26] during the period of Naik's leadership. For instance, Naik outperformed Welch, who increased the revenue and market value of GE manifold during his 20 years' tenure in the US. The revenue of GE rose from $26.8 billion to $130 billion with CAGR of 8 per cent for the period 1981–2001. The market value of GE increased from $14 billion to $410 billion for the same period with a CAGR of 13 per cent. Welch has a reputation of being one of the top CEOs of all time, and *Fortune* magazine even dubbed him 'Manager of the Century' in 1999.

On the other hand, during Naik's tenure as chairman in the period 1999–2019, the revenue of the L&T group of companies rose from about ₹5,000 crore to ₹1,60,000 crore, with a CAGR in revenue of 19 per cent.[27] Its market value increased from ₹5,800 crore to ₹2,80,000 crore with a CAGR of 21 per cent.[28] L&T did better than GE on both these parameters during Naik's leadership. In fact, the CAGR of revenue and market capitalization of L&T were higher than GE. L&T even outperformed Indian markets in terms

---

[25]This information can be found on L&T's website <https://investors.larsentoubro.com/StockInformation.aspx>
[26]For Sensex data, refer to <https://www.bseindia.com/market_data.html>
[27]Refer to L&T's website at <https://investors.larsentoubro.com/AnnualReports.aspx> (Accessed on 6 Nov 2019).
[28]Refer to L&T's website at <https://investors.larsentoubro.com/StockInformation.aspx> (Accessed on 6 Nov 2019).

of market valuation. Sensex for the period grew at CAGR—13 per cent against L&T's 21 per cent.

Naturally, shareholders were happy. But, how does one measure investors' delight? What would be the current value of investment in L&T's share of approximately ₹11,100 if invested in December 1999, when the share price was hovering around ₹555? Table 5.1 gives the return on investment that takes into account the rise in the share price and increase in the number of shares due to the bonus over the period from December 1999 to May 2019. The value of ₹11,100 invested increased to ₹2,75,400 in 20 years. The value of investment grew by roughly 25 times. The CAGR for the investment in L&T was 17 per cent against 11 per cent of Sensex. The calculation ignores the dividend income. If that is factored, the return on investment would be even higher.

Table 5.1
Measuring Return to the Investor

Date of Purchase/ Bonus Declared	Ratio of Bonus Declared[29]	Number of Shares Purchased (Post Bonus)	Market Price[30] (in ₹)	Value of Investment (in ₹)
Dec 1999		20*	555	11,100
July 2006	01:01	40	1,442	57,680
May 2008	01:01	80	774	61,920
May 2013	01:02	120	1,064	1,27,680
May 2017	01:02	180	1,256	2,26,080
May 2019		180	1,530	2,75,400

What is good for the stakeholder is good for the institution as per the Mindset–Behaviour–Action Grid. Naik was happy in his leadership role as he witnessed the results of his actions—be it creating capacities or turning L&T into a blue chip company in the course of his tenure.

Chapter 6 discusses Naik's attention to detail with regard to how he simultaneously nurtured organizational capabilities by creating verticals in the form of independent companies and also built a pipeline of leadership for the future.

---

[29]Refer to L&T's website at <https://investors.larsentoubro.com/StockInformation.aspx> (Accessed on 6 Nov 2019).

[30]Market price is BSE closing price on 31 December for each year. Available at <https://www.bseindia.com/markets/equity/EQReports/StockPrcHistori.aspx?expandable=7&scripcode=500510&flag=sp&Submit=G>

Chapter 6

Strategic Nurturing for Future Readiness

The secret of change is to focus all of your energy, not on fighting the old but building the new.

—Socrates

Shapers are multi-taskers. They operate at multiple levels. They invest their energies to build capacities for future expansion and globalization and simultaneously nurture a passion among employees to 'create value'. Their mind is preoccupied with concern for the future and sustainability.

Naik took several steps to shape and nurture the organization's capabilities to sustain it. He created 'independent companies' to streamline organizational structure by creating verticals and empowering leaders to function independently. He devised the strategy for making L&T future ready by capacity creation through Project Lakshya and by developing leadership via the Seven-Step-Leadership Development Process. He also evolved a succession plan for a transparent and well-calibrated transition for the organization.

TRANSFORMING BUSINESS

As chairman and at the helm of L&T, Naik worked to streamline operations, expand strategically, nurture leadership and make L&T future ready. He could see that over time various businesses of L&T had become bulky as the company went on expanding and diversifying in response to new opportunities. The international consultancy firm, McKinsey, was appointed as a consultant to suggest improvements in organizational structure. It was decided to simplify the structure and initiate a churning process. Businesses that were out of sync with the future were marked for rapid divestment. Naik led the process to streamline L&T's portfolio in 2012, and created 10 verticals of independent companies and six subsidiaries which would together run over 100 businesses. This was done to bring focus, accountability and autonomy. The idea was to reduce the complexity of the organization. Strategic thinking teams were formed and portfolios of activities were reviewed. The consultants introduced a new set of management vocabulary as they focused on 'restructuring', 'scalability' and 'shrink to grow' in a drive towards rationalization of a portfolio of activities.

Three directions were set. The first was the strategy of restructuring that was key to creating a lean organization. L&T divested from cement, cement machinery, glass container businesses, dairy, L&T–John Deere, L&T–Niro, Tullow India, L&T–Ramboll consulting engineers, and other non-core assets.

The second strategy was to expand and consolidate its international businesses. The company thus flagged West Asia and China as its predominant markets. The reasons were obvious: West Asia because it would allow it to leverage and extend its hydrocarbon, power transmission, infrastructure and heavy engineering clout and China because it was the fastest growing economy of the world for more than two decades at the time. It was a conscious decision to learn from both these geographies to leapfrog into other regions. Later, however, L&T withdrew from China and focused its attention on other geographical areas such as East Asia and West Asia.

The third strategy was to change the organizational structure by creating separate verticals.

CHANGING ORGANIZATIONAL STRUCTURE BY CREATING INDEPENDENT COMPANIES

All businesses and activities went through a review process. It was decided that whatever was found to be scalable and profitable should be grown by creating separate verticals. A list of verticals was made. These included: (*i*) power, (*ii*) hydrocarbon, (*iii*) machinery and products, (*iv*) heavy engineering, (*v*) infrastructure, (*vi*) buildings and factories, (*vii*) minerals and metals and (*viii*) electricals and automation. This list of verticals remained dynamic; some were merged and new verticals such as defence and realty were added. These independent companies had separate leadership and supported an exclusive board. The idea underlying the creation of verticals and independent companies was to separate entities and profit centres that would allow the leaders of these verticals to grow. By giving a leader complete autonomy over a vertical, Naik encouraged their entrepreneurial spirit.

In Venkataramanan's opinion, 'The strategy to split was to bring decision making closer to the businesses and to meet industry requirements.' The decentralization of power and autonomy allowed Naik to create a set of new leaders with a sense of ownership to operate efficiently and grow the verticals. The idea was to help develop a better leadership pipeline and attract lateral talent. The process to empower the leaders was so well entrenched in the system that whenever a proposal for a new project or a new investment was taken to Naik, his first question was always, 'Who is going to be the leader?' For him, leadership was of paramount importance. Only after studying the credentials and appraising the calibre of the one who would head the project, would he say, 'Yes, I would invest in that leader.'

When the consultants developed a structured process of managing the change, it was the team of top management who implemented it meticulously. Creating independent companies within the umbrella of L&T was a great move for transforming businesses. SNS shared an experience of how ECC was restructured into independent companies—building, transportation, water, heavy civil work, power transmission, and so on. He explained with the example of hiving off water as an independent company. He said, 'When you looked only at water, you could realize what the water business could become. What are the other water companies in the world? What they do in terms of technology? How can we geographically expand? How do we protect ourselves from changes in the environment? A leader was able to evaluate and assess several questions when his focus of attention was only water. The leader of each independent company developed by focusing only on his company and what he needed to do to grow, instead of bothering about other segments of this huge enterprise. Tremendous growth was registered from this concept.'

These independent verticals were set up with the objective that at a later date, each of these verticals could be listed on the stock exchange or sold. Infotech, technology services and financial services were listed, whereas the process to initiate exit of its non-core businesses, such as electrical and automation, is underway. Cement had been sold earlier in response to the takeover threat.

Although separate, the verticals converged under the broad umbrella of L&T that provided centralization of administration to this world of decentralized independent companies. The business heads would report to the CEO of L&T and its board would continue to reign supreme. Synergies would continue to be derived across businesses through key account management and shared revenues. Most importantly, it would lead to higher value creation for all stakeholders. L&T continued to be a hybrid holding company with several subsidiaries. The restructuring of L&T did not have any impact on reporting the financials that continued to be on a consolidated basis.

Naik's success in incubating new businesses is borne out by the fact that a large percentage of the L&T of today has been built from the ground up by him. He built Hazira in the face of internal doubt and opposition. He conceived Project

Lakshya to build new capacities in a planned and systematic manner under his leadership.

PROJECT LAKSHYA: IMPLEMENTING THE VISION

Lakshya is an acronym where each letter stands for a transformation brought about by Naik. The letter L stands for 'Lean', a structure that was changed from bulky and bureaucratic to lean; A stands for 'Agile', swiftly responding to threats and opportunities; K stands for 'Knowledge'; S for 'Speed and Scale'; H for 'Humane'; Y for 'Yielding Value'; and A for 'Action Orientation'. The acronym summarizes the philosophy and vision that governs L&T. It also sets the path for L&T to become a world class Indian MNC that is agile enough to take on emerging opportunities.

The primary aim of Project Lakshya has been to implement 'Big Projects' with a 'Broad Vision' that could transform L&T into a world class manufacturing company. The project was started with a perspective plan for 10 years with the top 300 people in the company to decide 'where the company should be in the future?' Project Lakshya provides the vision for focusing the energy of the company towards the creation of mega projects with a time-frame of five years, that is broken into yearly targets and further into quarterly targets. The target numbers and achievements are shared with SEBI and the stock exchange for complete transparency and accountability. L&T undertook the creation of mega facilities through Project Lakshya-I (2005–10), Lakshya-II (2010–15) and Lakshya-III (2016–21). Through Project Lakshya, L&T attained the status of an Indian MNC.

Implementation of the project provides a succinct example of achieving 'macro vision and micro planning.' Naik looked at this kind of planning and execution as an important exercise for transforming L&T to weather cycles of boom and bust. India's corporate watchers and investors acknowledged that L&T's core businesses had 'hit a sweet spot.' The company received due respect when Naik sharpened the focus of the company.

When Naik was asked, 'How do you think about so many mega projects in so many locations?' he provided a detailed answer, which in fact is the core of his strategy. 'Many people can think, some can conceive, few can strategize, but very few can make it happen. It is important to liberate your own self and the organization from the constraints of convention. It is not sufficient to exploit the current rules of the game to stay ahead of the competition. It is important to re-set the game and speedily secure first-mover advantage, while leaving the competition far behind.'

Naik is a stickler for details and follows a six-layered path: starting with a broad vision, he conceives, strategizes and plans for the implementation, following it up with a detailed plan replete with commas and full stops. What remains then is to implement the plan, get things done and see the results.

Under Project Lakshya, the broad vision for each project is identified. For example, Kattupalli was identified as the right location to set up the shipbuilding yard and the Modular Fabrication Facility to cater to Southeast Asian markets. L&T's success with Hazira in catering to countries west of India enthused the company to extend this opportunity to the eastern side as well. The first step always starts with project evaluation, especially based on parameters such as 'Return on Capital Employed (ROCE)' and 'Economic Value Added (EVA)', followed by land acquisition, project planning, architectural planning, blueprints, budgeting, sourcing of finance, material and machinery acquisition, manpower planning and training, and finally providing facilities for housing people and developing townships. Only when all these steps are followed meticulously does the vision turn to reality.

Several projects that were conceived and executed under Project Lakshya are now a reality. Although Hazira was created before Project Lakshya was initiated, it was enhanced and expanded under this project. New capacities were created at Bengaluru and Mysuru in Karnataka, Kattupalli and Coimbatore in Tamil Nadu, Vadodara and Hazira in Gujarat, Ahmednagar, Talegaon and Navi Mumbai in Maharashtra, Pithampur in Madhya Pradesh, and Puducherry. Spotting and acquiring the right location is always a key ingredient of any project, and Naik was an expert in this field.

As Mukhija said, 'Naik is adept at locating the right land parcel for the right purpose. He spotted the land in almost all places that included expansion of projects at Powai, Hazira, Coimbatore, Lonavala and many other facilities. His vision in terms of selection and use of the land resource is extraordinarily sharp.'

For instance, Powai in Mumbai was a marshland 70 years ago. But following the expansion of the city, Powai has emerged as one of the premium locations for residential and commercial complexes. Consequently, the price of land in and around Powai has also increased manifold. Mukhija recalled, 'Naik did the cost-benefit analysis on the back of an envelope and concluded that it was a waste of precious land resource and the workshop should be relocated to Hazira or any other location and free the expensive land for realty.' The process of shifting the manufacturing facility out of Powai has started. Plans are underway to develop the area with housing complexes, commercial buildings, schools, hospitals and a network of connecting roads.

READY FOR FUTURE CHALLENGES AND OPPORTUNITIES

L&T is readying itself for both challenges and opportunities in the future. The role of digital technology in infrastructure space in the future is expected to expand. For instance, in the smart infrastructure space, L&T has won a contract from the Government of Rajasthan to make Jaipur a smart city. SNS said, 'In my view, it is the first example of smart infrastructure, and in a sense, it changes the way people look at governance. This is an area where L&T has great potential to grow as we are already building infrastructure.' Naik was happy to note, 'When India moves to a digital future, L&T will be ready with the capability and commitment to build a smart world.'

Technology and defence are the next big areas identified as growth areas at L&T. Given their immense potential, Naik entered the defence and aerospace businesses nearly 30 years ago. Jayant V. Patil, who now leads the company's defence business said, 'there's much room for growth, whether they are howitzer field guns developed by Samsung, or submarines.'

Defence is a niche area and the competition is sparse.

Naik explained: 'After the defence production opened up, many companies sprung up in India. But it is not everyone's cup of tea. L&T has the expertise and deep knowledge of the subject. As a result, I expect the defence business to be 10 times its current size in the next five years.'

Technology lies at the heart of Lakshya 2021 with the company's strategic five-year growth plan for 2016-21. Naik affirms: 'We will be the technology leaders in our businesses and as a technology-led company we shall focus only on cutting-edge, high-tech and extremely complex projects that few other companies will attempt—space first, nuclear second, defence third and finally smart cities. Even the engineering and construction division will look at complex projects and not just at simple construction projects.'

SNS is passionate when he speaks of the new tech business—Smart World Communications. He believes this business will propel L&T as a key player in a sector dominated by the likes of Cisco and Juniper. He is convinced that L&T has a lead over other players in three key areas, namely, security solutions, smart communications and smart infrastructure.

GROOMING TALENT AND NURTURING LEADERSHIP

Naik has always been extremely good at spotting talent besides developing and nurturing it to transform into leadership. His emphasis on HR and the nurturing of human capital triggered major initiatives at L&T to attract, groom and retain talent, since the early days even before he took up the key leadership position. Venkataramanan recalled, 'Naik would carry people's files with him. He would think of who would go where and find the right situations to fit the right person in the right position. He was a great identifier of talent, and he could see what that person would do five years from then. Identifying talent, developing and nurturing it was his passion.'

As chairman of Indian Institute of Management Ahmedabad (IIM-A) during the period 2012–16, Naik endeavoured to develop the institute to become an outward-looking global management institute. He played a key role in bringing Ashish Nanda, a scholar from Harvard University, to IIM-A. On one of his trips to the US, Naik visited Nanda, convinced him to resign from Harvard Law School and take charge of IIM-A. He went out of his way to procure talent.

Naik often said that his management mantra for identifying talent was simple. 'If the person has devotion, passion, conviction and commitment—half the job is done. For the rest of the capabilities, a person can be groomed.' Naik made another strong point: 'Not many have the devotion. Everybody does hard work, but that is to maintain the job. If you are dedicated, you might add some value, but if you are devoted, you will multiply value.' Speaking about projects and people, Naik said 'I have satisfaction in two areas of my career at L&T—executing the projects from concept to reality and Human Resource Management. Thirty per cent of my time was spent on HR function.'

Naik's leadership and his love for the HR function is often compared with Roger Enrico, CEO of PepsiCo, who led the company through the high-stake 'Cola Wars' of the 1980s. Indra Nooyi, the CEO of PepsiCo from 2006 to 2018, described Enrico as 'a risk-taker, never afraid to challenge the status quo or make bold moves to get ahead. He was tough as nails, always prepared to get the job done and beat the competition. At the same time, he had a true love for our people and a passion for empowering them to reach their full potential.'

While L&T as a company has grown organically, talent growth in the company has also been organic. In this kind of professional environment, to bring about a cultural transformation and allow in-house talent to flourish was a huge task. Naik took up the challenge as he did in his early days during the workshops. He still follows the same principles and practices in the C suite.

Naik's HR policies incorporated a hard look at in-house talent and tried to solve two issues. One, he was acutely conscious of the fact that a lot of young people would rather choose IT or finance and not engineering. Talent drain was India's biggest problem. Previously, the drain was because the talent was going abroad. Now it is due to talent being employed in the outsourcing industry within India. Second, many bright young people left when L&T became a seniority-driven company. Naik changed the strategy. He said, 'Find the stars and bring them upwards straightaway. We must reward talent and promotions should be based on performance rather than seniority. In the next three years, they have to become the backbone of L&T. Our internal processes, training and development, encouragement and empowerment must enable ordinary people to do extraordinary things.'

He was 'deep diving' into his own junior levels to see what he had in stock before he started to recruit laterally. 'We want to be systematic about succession planning for each of the independent companies. For now, we want to take an inventory of future talent,' Naik said. This line of strategic thinking in terms of leadership development gave birth to the Seven-Step Leadership Development Process.

Seven-Step Leadership Development Process

The in-house leadership training programme at L&T has been Naik's pet project. This is the Seven-Step Leadership Development Process, a programme that is especially structured to bring out the best in an individual. The leadership development process is conducted in collaboration with reputed Indian and international business schools, and is customized to empower employees at different levels in the organization. What is interesting is that this process fulfils the specific needs of leaders at different levels within the organization. For example, the First-level Leadership Programme nurtures leadership skills for the front-line high potential employees. There are separate programmes designed for mid-level and senior managers at the threshold of stepping into a business leader's role.

The comprehensive Seven-Step Leadership Development Process was established to enable the development of a robust pipeline of leaders with a truly global mindset to meet the demand for leaders at the helm of different verticals of L&T.

1. *Management Education Programme:* An exclusive L&T and IIM-A collaborative programme, designed to groom young leaders, up to the age of 32 in the discipline of general management.
2. *Leadership Development Programme:* This programme, designed by L&T's Corporate HR, provides learning and

development for middle management, up to the age of 40. It focuses on the field and helps high-performing executives to assume leadership responsibilities.

3. *Global Leadership Development Programme:* Customized and facilitated by the Ross School of Business, University of Michigan, this programme is meant for participants in the age group of 40–50 years. It focuses on leadership skills for effectively competing in the global context.

4. *Transforming L&T into a Global Corporation:* Conducted in association with INSEAD, France/Singapore, and designed for top management executives in the age group of 40–50 years, the programme covers strategic choices including mergers and acquisitions, risk management and leadership attitudes from a global perspective.

5. *Global CEOs Programme:* Conducted by professors from Harvard Business School, it is targeted at leaders handpicked for future roles such as CEOs, business heads, board members and business leaders. The suggested age group is 55 years or less.

6. *International Executive Education*: Enterprising leaders are nominated for Advanced Management Programmes (AMPs) that are offered by selected globally renowned business schools such as the London Business School, Harvard Business School, Wharton School of the University of Pennsylvania, INSEAD, IMD (Switzerland), Saïd Business School and Oxford University.

7. *Mentoring*: A structured internal mentoring process by the Group Executive Chairman is instituted for senior executives, independent company heads and potential heads.

Throughout this training period, Naik played a crucial role in mentoring the candidates. An executive's metamorphosis into a leader was not complete until Naik personally mentored him. The candidates were enunciated into a centrality of 'People Power', as people are central to L&T's activities, achievements and the value it delivers to its stakeholders. The zeal, dedication and expertise of its people powers L&T's growth and prospects.

Most of the members of the current leadership team of L&T have benefitted from being groomed and mentored by Naik. Characteristically, thinking ahead of time, he has engaged with over 25 top executives to ensure that L&T has a robust leadership pipeline as far as 2040. Naik is happy to report, 'Five directors on the executive board have come out of this mentoring process, and seven persons have become CEOs of subsidiary companies or joint venture companies.' He started another batch of 29 for mentoring between the age of 35–45 to see that the pipeline of leaders is ready and L&T is in safe hands till 2040.

With over 65 per cent of the workforce below the age of 35, L&T is a young engineering conglomerate. A stimulating environment is provided for this young intellectual capital that includes a healthy mix of opportunity, responsibility, growth and purpose. The integrated talent management framework is established on a robust model that enhances employee capabilities and nurtures both professional and behavioural competencies. The work culture empowers individuals with the freedom to think beyond the conventional, innovate out of the box and raise performance levels.

SUCCESSION PLANNING

The thrust on leadership and grooming in-house talent has helped L&T overcome a hurdle common to many companies, that is, the pangs of succession planning. As Naik said, 'I have always believed that succession planning is vital for an organization's sustainability.' The transition to being the successor for Naik's position was planned well in advance.

Naik had spotted SNS, more than a decade ago and observed him while he was handling the construction business of L&T. His skill of planning and executing as well as his endurance was well established as he successfully handled large projects. The construction of major international airports in India and abroad; metro systems in Doha, Riyadh and multiple cities across India; and the Hi-tech City and Exhibition Centre in Hyderabad were among the projects managed by SNS. Over and above technical expertise and project management skills, SNS was groomed for the leadership role through the leadership development process and personal mentoring.

SNS shared a story about how a deal was closed for Delhi airport, a $2 billion project with the client GMR, with a lot of caution. SNS said, 'GMR was a young group then and L&T was worried whether they would be able to finance it.' SNS had done all the preliminary work and also taken care of the negotiations. When it came to closing the deal, Naik said, 'Let me talk to the board.' He bought some time and managed the event well. He went into another room and sat down as he felt that the magnitude of the decision was so big, you couldn't rush into it. It was settled later that day. As SNS said, 'I learnt a lot from that meeting with GMR and the way in which Naik handled it. That was when we came closer.' Naik took this opportunity to mentor him, 'If there was an argument with the client, stay cool and clear.'

SNS was groomed to understand the diverse business portfolio of L&T and its strategy. Once, while discussing the businesses of L&T, Naik told SNS, 'You are good at handling major projects, but you don't know much about the IT business.' SNS readily agreed as it was true. SNS offered to relocate in the US in order to understand and develop the IT business. SNS eventually understood the IT business thoroughly when he met hundreds of clients, learnt the technology and developed insights of business 'on the job.' This was Naik's way of developing and mentoring the leader.

SNS slowly took over the important divisions. As early as 2014, Naik had indicated that SNS would be the likely successor, and three years in advance, Naik made a formal announcement about SNS. Eight months before the scheduled date, he announced the next CEO and MD. He chose this period to allow a smooth transition for internal and external stakeholders. It was an important message as the community of stock analysts was jittery about the stock with the change in leadership. Naik sent a strong message to the markets, 'L&T is business as usual, and will not face a rocky transition when Naik steps down next year.' The L&T Board publicly announced that on 1 July 2017, SNS would be promoted to CEO and MD. The transition was transparent and well-calibrated. It was a demonstration of mature leadership. It ranks among the smoothest examples of corporate succession in Indian industry. Naik passed the baton to SNS in a formal ceremony.

Naik nurtured the organization's capabilities in terms of creating manufacturing capacities and setting up leadership training processes that made the organization future ready. We look at his distinct leadership style in Chapter 7 and deduce the tenets of 'The Naik Way' of shaping institutions.

Chapter 7

The Naik Way

> Winners don't do different things,
> they do things differently.
>
> —Shiv Khera

Emerging through the intertwined stories of L&T and Naik are some key lessons on shaping institutions. Is it possible to generalize these traits to motivate young leaders? Is it possible to derive some universal principles of leadership that can be used by individuals and companies seeking a transformation? The key takeaways for the reader with regard to the definition of leadership and what Naik did to transform L&T, besides the importance of corporate and personal philanthropy, are summarized here. A simple definition of leadership is that it is the art of motivating a group of people to act towards achieving a common goal. What is the secret sauce that makes some of them transformational leaders, another name for a 'Shaper'? Naik's story in the context of L&T provides a number of signals about his transformational leadership. It was Naik who helped transform the company by creating a bright yet realistic vision of the future; he motivated and inspired his people to engage with that vision, managed to turn the vision into reality and even saw to it that a pipeline of future leaders were ready to take the torch further. (*See* Appendix: SPJIMR Shaper's Mindset-Behaviour-Action Grid).

WHAT IS LEADERSHIP?

Like Naik, history is replete with people without formal training in leadership, but possessing something innate that allows them to achieve what they do. Naik did what he felt was right, which may or may not have any precedent, but he had conviction in his path. This kind of leadership often paves the way for the formation of new theories. He often talked about the four qualities, 'passion, conviction, commitment and devotion' that he considers a prerequisite for being a good manager. Probably, these are the qualities that lift the manager to become the leader and finally take them to the level of a Shaper.

Although Naik never defined or articulated 'The Naik Way', we believe that it emerges through his story as a strong contender for new theories of leadership and management. What worked? What was the secret sauce? How did the leader evolve into a Shaper? These are important questions and food for thought. We think that the contributions of Naik that shaped L&T into one of the top 10 engineering and construction companies in the world need to be recorded.

The authors borrow from the popular titles in 'The Way'

series that provide inspiring management mantras. *Jack Welch and the GE Way*[31] and *The Toyota Way*[32] are good examples for this. They are very simple mantras, but the crux of the matter is that the art of leadership lies in implementing simple solutions to achieve great success. The statement, 'winners don't do different things, they do things differently'[33] applies as a common denominator to all titles.

Jack Welch's innovative, breakthrough leadership strategies as CEO helped GE transform into a highly productive, labour-efficient powerhouse. *Jack Welch and the GE Way* reveals the strategies that led to Jack Welch's stunning success. The celebrated leader's management principles: 'keep it simple', 'face reality', 'embrace change', 'fight bureaucracy' and 'use the brains of every worker' worked wonders.

The Toyota Way expounded the management principles for lean manufacturing by altering the manufacturing process. The principles are simple. By employing 'fewer man-hours' and holding 'less inventory', achieving 'the highest quality cars' with 'the fewest defects' became possible. These universal principles could be applied across industries and geographies, enabling businesses to compete on cost and quality.

It may seem that we are romanticizing, but in our view, 'The Naik Way' could well be a contender to creating new theories of leadership and management for Indian managers. What we observed while writing this story, are some distinct characteristics that Naik showed. These are simple traits but,

---

[31] Robert Slater, *Jack Welch and the GE Way* (McGraw Hill Education, 1999).
[32] Jeffrey Liker, *The Toyota Way* (McGraw Hill Education, 2004).
[33] Shiv Khera, *You Can Win: A Step by Step Tools for Top Achievers* (Macmillan India Ltd, 1998).

when put into practice, provide some management mantras that we would like to call 'The Naik Way'.

TENETS OF THE NAIK WAY

1. *Focus on Value Creation:* The raison d'être for any business is value creation. Creating value for consumers, society and the nation, and distributing it among workers and investors is the prime reason for its existence. At times the focus from this simple logic gets blurred, as it happened with L&T. In response to the takeover threat, Naik took the opportunity to align the objective of value creation in L&T. By focusing the organization's energy on value creation, he could transform L&T into a blue chip company. This served two purposes: first, it created a ring-fence that saved the company from potential predators; and second, it made the company agile and competitive enough to be ranked among the top ten companies in the world.
2. *Future Orientation:* The distinction between business leaders and Shapers become apparent when one compares the way they perceive and respond to the challenges of the future. A Shaper is able to decipher emerging trends and future value drivers by restructuring the existing businesses and entering new ones. A Shaper builds an organization's capabilities by creating physical capacities and nurturing the human capital to be future ready. Naik paid attention to building capacities through his project Lakshya and nurtured leadership by the Seven-Step-Leadership Development Process.
3. *Translating Macro Vision to Micro Reality:* Mukesh

Ambani, chairman of Reliance Industries speaking at a public function said, 'Vision without implementation is illusion. Naik Saheb can take his team along and ensure that his vision is always implemented.' How did Naik plan at the macro level and execute at the micro level? Mukhija said, 'Naik's capacity to think in macro terms was amazing. If L&T had a huge capacity to cater to the Western world from Hazira on the western coast of India, it was necessary to build on the eastern coast as well. Kattapulli, on the eastern coast was the result of such macro thinking. At the same time, his attention to details is so great that he would micro-plan each process.'

How micro can you get? Naik would go down to the last decimal. Nothing escaped his attention—neither any number nor long-term implication of a current transaction. He could often recollect from memory the financial figures of almost all the businesses within the company.

4. *Raising the Bar and Scale of Thinking:* Shapers are neither content with their achievements nor do they dwell in the glory of their past laurels. At the customary function to mark the completion of any project, Naik's eye would inevitably turn to the next target, the bigger challenge. It is by constantly raising the bar that he was able to sustain his spiralling record of achievements which include raising value, enhancing talent, elevating levels of productivity, and remaining on the front-line of a constantly evolving business.

The bar is also raised when it comes to scale. While the rest of the company was talking about projects of ₹10 crore or thereabouts, Naik would shake them all up with a target of ₹50 crore or ₹100 crore. When Shapers set the benchmarks, they widen the horizons of all those whom they influence down the line. Soon, the others are ready to step out of their respective comfort zones and everyone in the team is thinking of scale.

5. *Value for Values:* In an industry's scramble for market share and desperate push for profits, businesses often face a dilemma—should we compromise on our values or miss out on a lucrative opportunity? Some managers may be swayed but Shapers stand firm and resolute. For them, the core values of the organization are inviolable. No cutting corners, no questionable practices—they play by the rules. As Naik put forth at an interview: 'The company's remarkable growth was achieved without deviating at any stage from its core principles and values.'

6. *Learner's Mindset:* The theory of the 'Growth Mindset' by Carol Dweck[34] says that people with a growth mindset have a learner's mindset. They are lifelong learners. Naik belongs to this category. He learned a great deal from the environment in which he operated. He did not read many books, instead he learned mainly from observation, interaction and questioning. He minutely observed people around him. During his business meetings, he would observe every person he shook hands with. He would observe, the way people approach a situation, the methods they follow, their strong points, and so on. This village boy learnt business etiquette by observation. He

---

[34]Carol Dweck, *The Mindset: The New Psychology of Success* (Random House, 2006).

was never shy of asking questions. He learned a great deal from workers, colleagues, and especially the IIT boys.

Describing Naik's learnability, Mukhija said, 'Naik had mastered diverse subjects by being a lifelong learner. He knew more about finance than a CA or CFO, more about law than a lawyer, more about the construction of structures and buildings than an architect and engineer. He had also mastered human resource management and entrepreneurship.'

7. *Openness and Humility:* When Naik took up the leadership position of CEO in 1999, he was aware of the gaps that needed to be filled to transform the company. In pursuit of the mission to transform L&T into a world-class conglomerate, there was a need for a long-term vision. He followed a participatory process and took feedback from employees at all levels. He valued insights from the people who were hands-on, and this reflected his great humility. To his employees, he asked a simple and direct question, 'What do you think we need to do to transform the company?'

Though he knew the pulse of the company and understood the pain points, he was open and keen to seek professional help from the best in the world. He called in top notch consultants such as McKinsey, BCG and Bain & Co. to achieve the goal of turning L&T into a world-class company. Naik intuitively understood that when one follows a systematic, structured process for change, the results would be phenomenal, and the margin of error would drastically reduce. He had the humility, discipline and openness to follow the suggestions made by the consultants. Despite having an experience of more than four decades in the company, he did not behave like a macho cowboy who could handle everything on his own.

Naik had made a resolve to learn every day since the beginning of his career. In his words, 'Every evening I reflect and go through my day, what have I done, how could I have done it better. It works on my mind, and the next day I try to do it differently.' This was his daily intention to learn and change that he practised diligently. Change management was embedded in his system.

8. *Leadership by Example:* Naik is exacting, and while he set tough targets for the team, he framed even tougher targets for himself. He would never ask anyone to do a task that he himself would not do. He would not confine himself to the comfortable air-conditioned room of a corporate office when his team was working in the trenches. He would be on the shop floor, at the project site and at the scene of action. Whenever there was a challenge, Naik would invariably be leading from the front.

Venkataramanan and Naik were both intensely involved in the construction phase of the Hazira project, from site selection to planning to execution—all of which required keen attention. For the first three years of the project, as previously mentioned, neither took their weekly day offs. Venkataramanan would sometimes feel tired but how could he complain when Naik too never took a day off in this period. Leading by example was Naik's leadership style.

9. *Building Personal Relations:* Naik interacted with everyone as if they were his family—be it workers, office staff or even

village activists. His relationship was at first-person level. He did not look down upon people from the position of power. He was direct and honest in his communication with people. If he did not approve, he would not hesitate to tell them so. If someone was hurt, he would call the person and talk with them in order to mend personal relations.

Gifted with a good memory, Naik would remember the names of the people whom he met in India or overseas. The most difficult must have been German names, but he would also remember the names of the Germans whom he had met 20 years ago! He would also recall when and where they had met. This enviable personal quality helped him create a great rapport with others, including foreigners.

Naik also always communicated with people using their name. Anyone who came in touch with him felt close to him and shared a great rapport due to this personal touch. Workers and union leaders felt privileged that the boss knew them personally. We wonder how many of us even bother to know the names of the watchman in our society or the tea boy at our office.

10. *Inspiring Large Audiences:* Soon after Naik took over as CEO, he went on a tour of L&T's large campuses across the country. The mission was critical—to make an organization of 40,000 people think, feel and act as one. Naik's method was simple—where there was doubt and uncertainty, he offered clarity; where there were multiple opinions, he presented a single, unifying stance; and most importantly, he won the hearts and minds of his audiences.

Naik spoke from the heart. There was a clear, compelling logic underlying all his speeches. He would not soft-pedal or beat around the bush. In fact, he continues to wow audiences at company get-togethers, the annual general meetings and industry forums.

11. *Work–Life Integration:* Naik worked long hours, often 16 hours a day without any weekly off, throughout his life. The term 'work–life balance' is commonplace today, but he felt that a person's time and life cannot be compartmentalized. To him, the concept of 'work–life integration' made more sense. He works tirelessly, never lets his guard down or his razor-sharp concentration get diffused. Yes, relaxation is vital as it could affect the quality of output, and Naik does relax, but his method of relaxation is to work some more!

    Naik's working style has set a trend. Others in the company have tried to emulate him. They too try to achieve a different interpretation to work–life balance. Naik initiated an environment in L&T where the wives also felt included. As Venkataramanan said, 'At L&T, the wives were proud of their husband's great work, and they created a social network that supported each other and in turn also their husbands!'

12. *Shared Prosperity the ESOP Way:* The professional management in L&T during Naik's term offered employees stock options. This is known as Employee Stock Ownership Plan (ESOP). The IT companies had already popularized the concept of ESOPs in India, but L&T was the first company from the old economy to do so in India. With the growth in revenue and profits, their

share price also grew. This benefited the employees as they too had a share in the prosperity. This created for the first time millionaires from the middle class. Naik was happy as he said, 'Everyone was retiring more prosperous.'

PHILANTHROPY

A concern for social and welfare issues complemented Naik's keen business interests. He was instrumental in setting up the L&T Public Charitable Trust, which undertakes a wide spectrum of community development work including skill training at several locations around the country. The multi-specialty hospital in Mumbai known as Nirali A.M. Naik Charitable Health-Care Facility, is fully functional and a boon for many in the vicinity.

Naik remains deeply committed to the community. He has pledged 75 per cent of his wealth to social causes in various sectors such as healthcare, education and skill development. He shares his family dynamics, 'If my son and daughter-in-law don't come back to India, then after me, a good part of the balance will also go to charity. They don't need the money. They encourage me to give it away. They have never objected to my decisions and always supported me in my plans.'

Healthcare

Following the Nirali Memorial Medical Trust named after his grand-daughter, Naik has also set up hospitals in Powai, Surat, Kharel and Vadodara. These hospitals are equipped with state-of-the-art facilities. Bearing in mind that many needy patients come from far-off places, many centres offer accommodation facilities for family members. A residential colony was also built for doctors, nurses and paramedical staff on the same premises wherever possible. Care was taken to set up training centres for the paramedical staff who provide quality support to the hospitals.

The Nirali Memorial Medical Trust has joined hands with Tata Trust to set up a comprehensive cancer care hospital at Vadodara. While the Nirali Trust would build the hospital infrastructure, set up advanced facilities and install state-of-the-art equipment, the Tata Trust would assume the responsibility for patient care and day-to-day operation. In addition to the cancer hospital, the plan is to build over the next five years, a general hospital, an eye hospital and a nursing college, all in Gujarat, Naik's *janmabhoomi* or birthplace.

Education

Education shapes the future of society. It exerts a decisive influence on individuals at the formative stage of their lives. The A.M. Naik Charitable Trust promotes education to meet multiple objectives. The trust promotes education by setting up schools in rural and urban India, laying special emphasis on the girl child.

Along with fostering modern education, the trust also helps to re-kindle respect for India's traditional values among the youth. The trust has been associated with Shri Muktananda Sanskrit Mahavidyalaya in expanding a unique institution, Shanti Mandir, at Mangod near Valsad, Gujarat. Within the larger precincts of Shanti Mandir, the trust has built

Geeta Vaidik Gram, a 16,000 sq. ft campus that encompasses the best of the ancient and the modern world. Classrooms and accommodation for faculty and students resemble the traditional *gurukul* while modern technology is evident in the state-of-the-art laboratories, science centres and computer centres.

The charitable trust has also built schools in Endhal and Kharel in Gujarat, and provided educational facilities across the region so that children from the poor sections of the society are offered the opportunity to study. Active assistance is provided to a number of educational institutions in three talukas of south Gujarat—Navsari, Chikli and Gandevi.

Skill Development

The A.M. Naik Charitable Trust views philanthropy as a focused and purposeful initiative. The broad spectrum community development initiatives of the trust include skill building in technical trades for school dropouts allowing them to become electricians, agromechanics, fitters, welders, carpenters, masons, and so on. Vocational training for women includes courses on beauty, tailoring and cooking, as well as starting other small businesses. There is also training on community service and rural development, assistance to farmers' co-operative, and training and development of teachers and technical staff. Naik realized that skill deficit is a major road block in society's path to progress. Besides helping develop technical skills, the training centres also help build soft skills and develop self-confidence, hope and positivity.

Naik has put in place a robust mechanism to ensure that every philanthropic initiative, whether a hospital or a school, is equipped with training centres for the staff. He uses his engineering and management skills to regularly monitor these projects and ensure that they achieve stated targets. He is committed to complete two projects every year. He follows L&T's ideology of 'concept to reality in terms of project execution' to make his philanthropic projects world class.

Recognizing Naik's contribution in the area of training and skill development, the government appointed him as chairman of the National Skill Development Corporation (NSDC). The skill ministry and the government believe that Naik's experience and leadership would help the 'Skills Mission' to achieve scale and bring in a larger industry connect. In 2018, the Minister for Skill Development, Dharmendra Pradhan, said, 'Naik's standing in the community of industry leaders would strongly enhance industry connect. His vast experience would take NSDC to greater heights. I'm confident that this organization under his leadership, apart from its engagement in executing skilling modules, should also be a think tank providing direction and necessary guidance to create a demand-based skilling ecosystem in the country.'

Epilogue

As co-authors we asked ourselves two questions: 'What did we set out to do?' and 'Have we really accomplished it?'

We set out to make a distinction between a company and an institution. We set out to make a distinction between a manager, a leader and a Shaper. We set out to make this distinction in an engaging way and hope this piece of research fulfils it. Perhaps, driven by the desire to have a closure to this narrative, we write this epilogue.

We started this inquiry by asking, 'Who is a Shaper? Is he different from a business leader?' 'How does the Mindset, Behaviour and Action of an individual change as he evolves from a manager to a business leader to a Shaper?' In our research to understand how the three influence the destiny of the company over a long term, there emerged some interesting insights.

Prima facie, the three could be the same person at different stages of his/her career. However, we arrived at a nuanced understanding and the set of special qualities that are part of the secret sauce for the progression from a manager to a business leader to a Shaper. It is important to note here that the progression may neither be natural nor universal. All managers may not evolve into business leaders and all business leaders may not ultimately graduate into Shapers who bring about transformation in the organization. In all three roles, there is a vast difference in the Mindset, the Behaviour and the Action with reference to the 3Ps—Policy, Processes and People.

THE MANAGER

At the base level, the manager meticulously implements policies and attempts to meet the targets and solves all the routine problems. Managers streamline processes and remove obstacles for a seamless operation. Motivating people and managing them at the ground level is crucial at this stage.

THE BUSINESS LEADER

At the developmental level, the business leader makes policies, sets targets, allocates resources, co-ordinates between the different functions and works to achieve the company's vision. People management at this level is crucial by evolving clear policies for remuneration and reward through a process of review.

THE SHAPER

Finally, the Shaper operates at the long-term and structural level. The focus of attention changes from 'operations' to 'transformation of the organization to be future ready'. The focus shifts towards creating capacities, reorganizing and restructuring businesses. The Shaper becomes instrumental in developing a vision-mission statement that changes the trajectory of a company. The Shaper creates an environment of people participation that is inclusive and facilitates leadership development.

India needs business institutions and Shapers to realize her true potential at the current stage of development. This large mass of land that is home to one-sixth of the world's population has been anxiously waiting for transformation. Who would lead the country in this soul-elevating experience? Politicians are great force who are expected to shape the destiny of the country in India and elsewhere. However, in a democratic set up, their actions being subject to the vote bank, they often find it difficult to keep a balance between short-term pain and long-term gain. Moreover, they are often lost in the complexities of managing so many diverging constituents. As we were looking elsewhere to find a dependable and responsible entity who could be entrusted with this responsibility, business leaders emerged as the best choice. Businesses have acted as an engine for growth and development in the history of the US, Europe, Japan and even China. It is now India's turn to wholeheartedly connect to it.

The popular perception of businesses through the eyes of left-leaning politicians, economists, academics and journalists is that of greedy, power-hungry megalomaniacs. However, business makes most of the stuff that we enjoy. Business gives the nation jobs. It is humane, and a synonym for both opportunity and prosperity. Therefore, it deserves a higher status in society and should be respected for its virtues, even as it is striving to reduce its vices. The frauds in business are an extension of the propensity of society as a whole. Business practitioners stand as much on a pedestal as educationists, doctors, administrators and the defence forces.

Using the metaphor of an automobile, good vehicles require three attributes: first, an engine that can efficiently burn an energy-rich fuel into mechanical power; second, a transmission that delivers mechanical energy to the wheels; third, good brakes and a comfortable seat. Passengers must experience speed, comfort and safety in the car. However, the presence of these do not imply that there will never be a car accident. So it is with business.

This metaphor can be further extended to society at large. First, society needs aggressive, entrepreneurial people; they are like the fuel in the car. Second, the business energy must be guided with capabilities and infrastructure. In this context, the gears of the car are metaphors for education, health, housing and communications. Finally, just as a car needs brakes and shock absorbers, a society is also cushioned from shocks and volatility with the help of regulations, surveillance, and so on. Hence, the three components of a wholesome society are business, infrastructure and governance.

For the first 40 years after Independence till liberalization took place in the early 1990s, Indian businesses were regarded in society with suspicion. The underlying tone of government policies and social perception was 'catch the crook'. Over the next 30 years since liberalization, Indian businesses began spreading their wings in India as well as globally. The outcome is encouraging but it remains a mixed bag; some of them succeeded, some of them overstretched while some have failed miserably. However, this should be looked as a normal phase in the development of any country. In a competitive and vibrant society, free entry and free exit of businesses lead to an efficient society where all stakeholders benefit—be it consumers, workers, investors or entrepreneurs.

ROLE OF BUSINESS IN SOCIETY

Once we are clear about the role of business in our society, what we need is not just companies but business organizations that have transformed into business institutions. Business institutions are clear about their purpose. They have a vision, mission and philosophy that underlie their existence. The performance of these institutions is dependable as it is more durable and longer lasting. They nurture talent and strive to achieve efficiency and competitiveness. The transformation of companies as institutions is still at a nascent stage in India. We as a society need to nurture this activity. Creating and celebrating strong business institutions must become a national priority.

Business is a fabulous force for good in society, conducted by good people with good results for the national good. For example, Unilever, Tata and L&T have been highly ethical and responsible companies for about a century. They have done so with occasional displays of the human frailties that all of us are prone to. In fact, it is those occasional frailties that remind the observer that there are no gods in society—there are some outstanding people, many good people and a small number of misdirected people.

India needs great business leaders, but the time has come for India to nurture business Shapers if the national dreams for the economy are meant to fructify. If this is 'India's century', there lies a huge responsibility on the shoulders of business leaders to make transformational changes to shape their companies. They can make their business strong so that they can withstand the vicissitude of the economy and markets. They will require renovation and reinforcement from time to time.

We define the Shapers mindset through these 10 features that have theoretical underpinnings.

1. *Intuition and Skill*: Shapers are like surfers waiting for the big wave. They do not control the waves but can ride on them. They do not try to control events or structures, but can anticipate them and 'bend' them to their purpose to some degree. Just like waves that soon subside, events create windows of opportunity, which may close in a relatively short period. Many opportunities for change, like waves, may go untapped. Institutional leaders matter when they have the intuition and skills to take advantage of those 'waves', especially when they hit the shores, taking onlookers by surprise.[35]

2. *Out-of-the-Box Thinking:* Shapers are 'event-making' leaders rather than 'eventful' leaders. An eventful leader influences the course of subsequent developments by his actions. In Hook's metaphor, the mythical little Dutch boy who stuck his finger in a leaking dike and saved his

---

[35]Joseph Nye, *The Powers to Lead* (Oxford University Press, 2008).

country was an eventful leader, but any little boy or any finger could have done the trick. On the other hand, an event-making leader akin to Shapers, does not just find a fork in the historical road: he helps to create it. They raise new issues and new questions.

3. *Seeing the Big Picture:* Shapers are guided by 'institutional logic', rather than 'economic logic'. For our leaders, the economy is embedded in society. Therefore, social groups form the unit of analysis and not individuals. Individual decisions are grounded in a socially constructed view of the world and are motivated by social concerns.[36]

4. *Integrated Future Transformers:* Shapers are thoughtful leaders whose model of leadership is integrated. We believe that institutional leaders do three things consistently—they plan with vision and values, they organize with alignment and clarity, and they control with motivation and involvement. In this way, they amalgamate and synergize managing, directing and engaging in a way that not only serves as an integrated model, but also helps shape and expedite their movement into becoming future transformers.[37] In times of business uncertainty, Shapers compensate through institutional grounding and compatibility to institutional values. Most investment decisions are made with the intent of securing the future. Transmission of institutional values through investment on the people side ensures sustained

---

[36] Kanter and Khurana, 'Institutional Perspectives and Framework on Managing and Leading'.
[37] Fisher, *The Thoughtful Leader*.

competitive advantage, even though it may not be justified through immediate financial returns.[38]

5. *Imparting Core Values:* Shapers are sautéed in certain core values. They deeply believe that core values permeate the total being of both the institution and the institution builders. Shapers energize their people to internalize the organizational mission and values. Often, Shapers impart relevant values through personal relationships.

6. *Recognize Talent:* Institution builders or Shapers are focused on developing internal talent, rather than having to borrow from outside. Shapers intuitively spend a lot of time identifying talent, nurturing the best people and advancing their preparedness for greater responsibilities. This is a prominent and distinct behaviour of Shapers.

7. *Relationship Builders:* Shapers envision beyond strategy, structure and system as well as purpose, process and people. Rosabeth Moss Kanter refers to Indra Nooyi of PepsiCo as an institution builder after she tried to reshape the relationship between business and society through her efforts towards the environment and social change, such as partnering with a waste recycling company, focusing on agro-based industry, and so on.

8. *Detached Objectivity:* Shapers possess a detached passion that not only enables them to be passionate about ideas and goals but they also have the ability to take a few steps back and look at the organization, self and their own thinking and activities objectively, as it in the long-term

---

[38]Rosabeth Moss Kanter, 'How Great Companies Think Differently', *Harvard Business Review*, November 2011.

interest and sustenance of the organization. Ravi Mathai of IIM-A was an institution builder. He stepped down after six years as director to become a faculty although his appointment letter did not indicate his tenure as director. He believed that there was a need for fresh blood into the organization. He is known to have said: 'The building of an educational institution is often an act of faith, and the expression of that faith is in philosophy, based on which, those who build such institutions act.'

9. *Creators with Visionary View:* Shapers are pioneers, founders of institutions, ground-breakers, transformers and creators of new institutions. They create the overarching culture within the organization. They 'lay' the foundation. While most leaders 'build' on that foundation, a Shaper is like 'Brahma', the creator of the universe. Shapers are charismatic, bold and a greater visionary than a leader. However, there are some common traits between the Shaper and the leader. Both are driven by the objectives to carry forward the organization, inspire others, instil confidence and build high-quality teams.

10. *Tough Motivators:* Shapers are remembered more for their tough qualities than for softer qualities like empathy or genuine concern for others. Those who have been shaped recall Shapers as being tough people. In long-established companies, Shapers may change the trajectory based on the belief that an 'as is, where is' approach cannot succeed for long. Shapers do what is right for society. Leaders may have vested interests or they may cut corners. Monopolistic organizations do not readily qualify as institutions.

Appendix

Research Methodology Shaper's 'MBA' Grid

A section on research approach and methodology seems out of place in a practice-oriented book that aims to guide the modern-day manager and leader to be the Shaper of an organization, especially one who can outlive his/her peers and is hailed as an institution by virtue of his/her actions. While the book aims to be practitioner relevant, it is also true that this ambitious research project of studying six different organizations recognized as institutions in India, had to be guided by a theoretical construct that would be able to discern patterns. We term this theoretical construct as the 'Shaper's Mindset–Behaviour–Action (MBA) Grid' which is an important enough contribution, as it has the potential to act as a beacon for other researchers interested in and working in the field of leadership and organizational behaviour in the Indian context.

As such, we decided to 'relegate' the research approach and methodology to an appendix section, rather than use a book chapter for the same. The advantage of an appendix is that it can be skipped by those disinterested in the research approach itself without much loss of continuity in the narrative. At the same time, it seemed apt to present before serious researchers—who seek to further the research agenda on the theory and practice of institution building—a thorough understanding of the Mindset, Behaviour and Action patterns of institution builders.

Again, unlike a conventional research methodology section in an academic paper, we shall seek to keep this section light, highlighting the 'What', 'Why' and 'How' of our research in a language that will appeal to the lay reader, as much as to the seasoned academic.

SHAPERS RESEARCH PROJECT: THE 'WHAT'

The Shapers Research Project owes its genesis to a serendipitous discussion amongst a few SPJIMR faculty members in 2018 on the distinction between organizations and institutions, and the associated distinction between leaders of the two. Following some research, there were discussions over endless cups of coffee in the faculty lounge that veered around Indian companies in the Fortune Global 2000 list. There were about 50 that made the cut, such as RIL in the top 200 list and TCS in the top 500. There was a tentative consensus at this stage that not all these organizations were 'institutions'. While these organizations are aspirational to several MBA students who seek to find jobs within them, they offer little hope to the sceptic who is convinced about the mortality of corporations.

An influential piece of research in 2012 by Professor

Richard Foster from Yale University, posited that the average lifespan of a company listed in the S&P 500 index of leading US companies has decreased by more than 50 years in the last century, from 67 years in the 1920s to just 15 today.[39] Another study found the age of business survival to be merely 10 years.[40]

Given that most Indian businesses have emerged post the opening up of the Indian economy in 1991, yet they face multiple business challenges in the current uncertain and volatile business environment. The common question that emerged was: 'Which of these organizations will survive long enough? Which Indian businesses are institutions?'

At this stage, we defined the term 'institution', as one which had at its core certain universally accepted values and norms for which it was revered; it had withstood the test of time, having been established within a decade or two since Independence and seemed to possess an innate resilience to withstand multiple business challenges, having already survived several such challenges in the last several decades.

As we began to identify some of these organizations that qualified as institutions, we realized that in addition to some factors which distinguished them from others, we arrived at our Eureka moment at the realization that the phenomenon of institution-building is deeply linked to the leadership experience that each one goes through. In particular, we realized that the hypotheses for the research project, were it a conventional one, could very well read as follows:

---

[39]Refer to <https://www.bbc.com/news/business-16611040>
[40]Refer to <https://fortune.com/2015/04/02/this-is-how-long-your-business-will-last-according-to-science/>

H1: The number of years an organization will survive will be linked positively with leadership performance.

H2: The ability of an organization to withstand business volatility and severe business challenges will be linked positively to leadership performance.

H3: The reputation that an organization will carry will be linked positively to leadership performance. Needless to say, our preliminary research into institutions was guided by a literature review of scholarly work on institution building, ranging from Walter W. Powell, Arie de Geus, Paul J. DiMaggio, John W. Meyers and Brian Rowan to Indian scholars such as Udai Pareek.

This then led to the question: What sort of leadership performance will qualify for transformation of ordinary organizations into venerated institutions? The obvious answer was 'transformational' leadership of a sort that transcends the current notion of leadership, as enunciated by Daniel Goleman, Rosabeth Moss Kanter and others. Transformational leadership is one that not only transforms, but rather 'shapes' the organization into an institution. Such leaders may be called 'Shapers'. We also realized that just as there are few organizations that make it to a list of 'institutions', there are only few business leaders who may qualify as 'Shapers' of institutions.

This led us to an additional hypothesis:
H4: Leadership Mindset, Behaviour and Actions undertaken by Shapers are unique and distinct from those of the leaders.

We thought we were on to something interesting with

this discovery. The next obvious question was: could we, as a group of interested researchers, work on a set of Indian organizations that *we* could identify as institutions, using a commonly accepted set of parameters? The set of such institutions need not be exhaustive. However, they need to conform to the parameters laid out, and should not be questionable by the set of researchers working on the project, which now had a name—the SPJIMR Shaper's Project. Can such institution-building be studied in the context of the leaders, who as Shapers, shaped and created them in a manner such that they were enduring? Could we study and glean a set of uniform Mindsets, Behaviour and Actions, which would set these leaders apart from other leaders who were non-Shapers? And, how do these Shapers shape their organizations into institutions?

This then led to the second aspect of our research: Why did we want to do this?

SHAPER'S RESEARCH PROJECT: THE 'WHY'

Well, we could advance a large number of great-sounding explanations for why we undertook this research project. For example, 'We wanted to understand the mindset and actions of Shapers so that it can help create Shapers for the future.' Or, 'We want to make a difference to Indian management discipline and practice.'

These reasons are valid and good enough to conduct any such research. However, as every well-intentioned researcher in the field of social science will testify: We undertake research when the theme excites us. It helps us uncover a phenomenon that we have little understanding of and one that we wish to unravel. In the process, we help set the research agenda for others as well.

In this case, it made sense since we could discern hints of a pattern emerging, even as we began to do our preliminary research based on secondary data. We realized that rather than talking of leadership types in an anecdotal fashion, we could possibly decipher a method to such transformational leadership, not consciously agreed upon by those who practice it, but there all the same, waiting to be discovered and possibly even replicated.

In particular, what excited us were questions such as:

- How does one recognize an institution from an organization, even if the key metrics used to map organizational performance were similar, that is, involved deeper qualitative questions than merely looking at quantitative metrics? Thus, for instance, why should Reliance not feature in our list, even though it is one of the top Indian companies on the Fortune Global 2000 list.
- What transforms an organization into an institution? It is important to note here that the emphasis was on the process and not the outcomes.
- What Mindset, Behaviour and Actions set apart a leader from a Shaper? This would follow a deep qualitative analysis, which could form the basis for a new theoretical construct, called the 'Shaper Construct'.
- How and when does a leader qualify as a Shaper?

These questions also became the 'Why' or the 'Purpose' of our research, which is aimed at finding out why organizations and leaders are different. In this process, if we are able to expedite the transformation of some business organizations into institutions through their leaders adopting the right 'Shaper' mindset, that will be a happy, albeit unintentional, consequence of this book and project.

This leads us to our final question: How did we manage to undertake and bring this project to fruition?

SHAPER RESEARCH PROJECT: THE 'HOW'

The process of shortlisting the tentative candidate organizations for the research project was undertaken by R. Gopalakrishnan, the lead author, and Ranjan Banerjee, the Dean of SPJIMR. A set of six institutions were initially shortlisted, with the understanding that a second round of institutions could be worked upon at a later stage. The institutions shortlisted in the first round included, in alphabetical order: Biocon, HDFC, Kotak, L&T, Marico and TCS. The methodology we sought use in the project was a case study approach, involving in-depth interviews and triangulation. The project was then presented to the publisher, and approval was sought.

Each of the co-authors, well-respected academics in their own rights, began with carrying out background research on their subject of study—both the Shaper and the institution. At least one book in the series, the one on TCS, involved researching two Shapers for the same institution.

We deliberated, discussed and arrived at the idea of a 'Framework' that could be used to explore the main hypotheses.

This was named the SPJIMR Mindset-Behaviour-Action Grid. The contents of the grid itself were arrived at through an iterative process of refinement as the research progressed.

In the initial stage, the grid was visualized as a 9*9 matrix for managers, leaders and Shapers as distinct agents along task and process dimensions. The task dimensions considered were: Managing the Core; Preparing the Future; and Creating the Future. Along the process dimension, managers were hypothesized as focusing on policies and processes, leaders as focusing on performance while Shapers would focus on people. Juxtaposing the task and process dimensions, we arrived at a set of nine unique actions, which would set apart Shapers from leaders and managers.

In the second stage, we refined this further to arrive at an 8*3 matrix. The vertical dimension (the columns) looked at mindset, behaviour and actions, while the horizontal dimension (the rows) looked at these Mindset-Behaviour-Action Grid broadly based on the 4Ps: Purpose, People, Policies and Processes. A Shaper was identified in terms of his or her mindset along eight dimensions: people relations, short-term and long-term focus, critical thinking, orbit shifting, breaking barriers, levers of change, cyclical learning and stakeholder orientation. The Mindset-Behaviour-Action Grid is reproduced in Table I.

The final step was to seek in-depth interviews with the Shapers of the institutions they represented, as also with multiple stakeholders, who could shed light on various dimensions of the Shaper and the institution. While we decided and planned for the interviews, the idea was clear. The book was not meant to be a hagiography. Though there were protagonists within the case study approach who were the Shapers, the hero clearly was the institution, which had withstood the test of time and made a distinct contribution to nation-building. Again, it was a conscious decision not to discuss the warts and all of the Shapers. The reason is because we are interested in understanding the positive mindset of the Shaper, an individual who largely has an unblemished track record. Having said this, it is important to remember that the Shaper too is as human as any of us in terms of human frailties and vulnerabilities. Thus, nowhere should the book be construed as an attempt to idolize a human being with a larger-than-life image.

Each researcher conducted at least three such interviews with different people associated with the Shaper and/or the institution. Some of us met our protagonists more than once. The questions used to test the hypotheses included some generic questions, as well as some specific ones, particular to the institution and its Shaper. Some examples of questions revolving around institution-building are as follows:

- How did you set the organizational vision, values and performance expectations?
- How do you attract, retain and enhance talent within your organization?
- What is the leadership's purpose? How do you communicate with your workforce?
- How do you arrive at and institutionalize the core values of the organization?
- What is the role of 'out-of-the-box' thinking and entrepreneurial mindset for any organization? How do

you ensure that such a mindset gets internalized into the DNA of the institution?
- How do you and your senior leadership team guide and sustain the organization?
- How do you develop future leaders, measure organizational performance and create an environment that encourages ethical behaviour and high performance?
- What are the institution's core competencies, work systems and design that help to create value for your customers?
- How do you identify the organization's blind spots in achieving long-term organizational success and sustainability?
- What specific processes in institution-building have you undertaken?
- How have you addressed succession planning in your organization?

There were other questions pertaining to the Shaper, which sought to explore key facets in their life—starting from childhood, role models, and so on—that helped 'shape' the Shaper. Another interesting question posed to the Shapers was this: If they were given another three to five years at the helm, what would be the key 'unfinished' agenda they would want to address?

All these questions helped glean the Shaper's mindset, behaviour and actions relating to specific aspects of institution-building. We probed three specific areas: building the institution (sometimes from scratch), seeing it through troubled times and changing its course. The idea was threefold: understanding the context, understanding the leader and understanding the institution.

The chapters of this book have also been aligned accordingly. The initial chapters set the context in which the organization developed, while the next set of chapters look at the life and key influences on the Shaper, as also specific aspects of the Shaper's mindset, behaviour and actions. The last set of chapters in the book series covers the institution, including a discussion on what makes an organization qualify as an institution, salient features of an institution, and understanding the future of the institution.

Table I
SPJIMR SHAPER'S MINDSET–BEHAVIOUR–ACTION (MBA) GRID

Mindset	Behaviour	Action
People relations: Respectful to others	Sensitive and empathetic to others	Engages with people and nurtures them
Short versus long term: Both are equally important	Encourages to deal with the immediate while silently considering the long term	Acts on the immediate decisively to get results, creating the impression of small wins, so as to look forward to and work towards a big 'victory' in the future

Critical thinking: Considers options and their pros and cons in mental evaluation	Encourages discussion and debate with an open-mindedness	Acts with precision and demands accountability
Orbit changing: Constant evaluation of which orbit change will benefit the organization	Tosses around and debates the risks and rewards of orbit change, almost appearing indecisive	Demonstrates single-minded commitment once a decision is made
Break barriers: I have the freedom to act if I am willing to steer through obstacles	Identifies the obstacles and seek the best way to deal—break it, go around it, or navigate it	Once the path is clear, pursues with an Arjuna-like determination
Levers of change: Action is within my reach (Must change complacency to the aspirational mindset)	Debates and seek ways out to unlock the organization from negative hooks while attaching positive hooks	Presses for action and change in a disciplined manner
Cyclical learning: Action–Observation–Benchmark–Review–Act again	Insists on a systems approach of cyclical learning	Ensures organization-wide deployment of an accepted system

| Stakeholder orientation: What is good for the stakeholder is good for the institution and hence, for us | Constantly understanding customer and community perspective | Always acts by keeping in mind multiple stakeholder interests |

Acknowledgements

As co-authors of this book, we have laboured through it and as we review the fruits of our labour, we must first thank each other. Each of us has brought in our individual skills, but we hope that the book we have produced is not just the sum of our skills but greater than the sum. That would be the greatest tribute to our collaborative effort.

We must thank Dr Ranjan Banerjee, Dean of SPJIMR, in conceiving and supporting the Shaper's Project. We would also like to thank the faculty group with whom we have had opportunities to interact, which led to mutual help and pride among the cohort group. There has been institutional support for the research and enlightening interaction among the faculty. We had an atmosphere of curiosity where questions could be raised, debates were held and we hope that ultimately, we have produced some concrete output.

This book is part of the series of books where we have recognized the Shapers of business institutions who have created history in the current period. The purpose of this exercise is to highlight and improve on 'management thought leadership' and 'to develop a theory that can impact practice'. This exercise could be viewed as part of our commitment to the mission of SPJIMR to 'Influence Practice and Promote Value-based Growth'. Through the Shaper's Project, we have endeavoured to acknowledge and celebrate the Shapers who have transformed their organizations.

We are grateful to the entire Rupa team for their help on this project.

The heart of the book is in its content. We thank all those at L&T who gave us their time unstintingly. The conversations with people associated with L&T have given us a first-hand experience of the mammoth task at hand in transforming a company into an institution. We would like to thank them for expressing themselves with no holds barred and sharing their excitement in the journey. Naik's vision for the future and his macro view of the situation was a testimony to our belief that Shapers are a different breed. SNS too, expressed his views clearly and we could gauge the future readiness of L&T. A special set of thanks are due to the three veterans at L&T—K. Venkataramanan, R.N. Mukhija and V.K. Magapu. All three of them have brought to light the insights and mindset of Naik at different stages of his life due to their close proximity with him.

Special thanks are due to the team at L&T—P.R. Kothari, Advisor to the Group Chairman and Jairam Menon, Communication Consultant for their painstaking efforts to go through the manuscript and improve the quality of the narrative. Their suggestions have added immense value to the book. Shaily Trivedi's passion for the organization was evident as she, being EA to the Group Chairman, promptly connected us with various offices and almost owned the project.

Last but not least, we would like to thank our families

and friends who wholeheartedly supported us in this exercise. Be it our long hours of solitary confinement or issues with mounting tensions, they were there to support us. They read the manuscript at various stages and provided some timely and useful suggestions without which the book would not have been what it is.

Index

Aditya Birla Group, 59, 67
Ambani, Dhirubhai, 58
A.M. Naik Charitable Trust, 106, 107
Amul Dairy, 12
Azad, Abdul Kalam, 19

Bajaj, viii
BARC, *see also* Bhabha Atomic Research Centre, 18, 70
Bhabha Atomic Research Centre, *see also* BARC, 18
Birla, viii, 31, 59, 62, 64, 67
Birla, Kumar Mangalam, 59, 64
blue chip company, xiv, 66, 69, 76, 98
Bombay Stock Exchange, viii
Bossidy, Larry, xiii, 74
BOT, *see also* Build Operate Transfer 21, 22

British India, 1, 3, 7
Build Operate Transfer, *see also* BOT, 21
Build Own Operate Transfer, *see also* BOOT, 21

CAGR, *see also* Compound Average Growth Rate, 64, 65, 74, 75
Carnegie, Andrew, x
Carnegie Steel, x
Caterpillar Tractor Company, 9
Compound Average Growth Rate, *see also* CAGR, 64
corporate DNA, 56, 57
Corporate India, 73

Defence Research and Development Organisation, *see also* DRDO, 19

Desai, Mangaldas, 9
DRDO, *see also* Defence Research and Development Organisation, 19

Engineer, Procure, Construct *see also* EPC, 8, 16, 45, 46, 80
Economic Value Added, 84
Employee Stock Ownership Plan, 104
Engineering and Construction Corporation, 8
EPC, *see also* Engineer, Procure, Construct, 22

Federation of Danish Industries, 4
FERA, *see also* Foreign Exchange Regulation Act, 18, 20
First-level Leadership Programme, 89
F.L. Smidth & Co., 2, 15
Foreign Exchange Regulation Act *see also* FERA, 18

Gen-C institutions, viii
Gen-L institutions, viii, ix

Godrej, viii
Golden Quadrilateral project, 22
Green Revolution, 13
Growth Mindset, 100
Gujarat Narmada Valley Fertilizers Corporation, 14

Hazira, 46, 48, 49, 50, 51, 52, 53, 54, 55, 81, 83, 84, 85, 99, 102
heavy engineering, 17, 53, 79
Heavy Engineering Division, 18, 45
Hilda Ltd, 7
Holck-Larsen, Henning, xii, xiv, 1
Hydrocarbon Engineering, 45, 46

IADP, *see also* Intensive Agricultural Development Programme, 13, 14
import substitution policy, 11
Indian Space Research Organisation, *see also* ISRO, 19, 23, 70
Industrial Policy Resolution 1948, 10

Industrial Revolution, 2
institution, viii, ix, x, xi, xii, xv, 44, 76, 109, 119, 120, 121, 122, 123, 124, 125, 126, 127, 128, 129, 131, 134
institutional logic, 115
Intensive Agricultural Development Programme, *see also* IADP, 13, 14
Internet of Things, 72
Investor Delight, 73

Japanese Construction Consortium, 16
Jeejeebhoy, Sir Jamsetjee, 7

Kristian, Søren, xii, xiv, 1
Kurien, Verghese, 11

Leadership Development Programme, 89, 90
liberalization, viii, ix, 21, 70, 112
Licence Permit Raj, 42
L&T-John Deere, 78
L&T-Niro, 78
L&T-Ramboll, 78
Lump Sum Turn Key, 22

Magapu, V.K., 39, 51, 134

Management Education Programme, 89
manufacturing company, 6, 82
marshland, 48, 49, 84
Mindtree, 72
Modular Fabrication Facility, 53, 83
Mody, Sir Homi, 7
Monopolies and Restrictive Trade Practices (MRTP) Act, *see also* MRTP Act, 20
MRTP Act, *see also* Monopolies and Restrictive Trade Practices Act, 42
Mukhija, R.N., 54, 134

National Dairy Development Board, 12
National Fertilizers Ltd, 14
Nestor Boilers, 34, 35, 36
New India, 3
Nirali Memorial Medical Trust, 105

Operation Flood, 11, 12, 13
Orbit Changing Policies, 47

Polar Satellite Launch Vehicle, 23

Post-Reforms Period, 19
Powai, 11, 15, 41, 47, 49, 50, 84, 85, 105
PPP, *see also* Public Private Partnership, 21
price/earnings multiple, 69
profitability, 68, 69, 70, 72
Project Blue Chip, 66, 69, 70
Project Lakshya, 77, 81, 82, 83, 84
Public Limited Company, 11
Public Private Partnership, 21

Quit India, 25, 26

Rashtriya Chemicals and Fertilizers, 14
Return on Capital Employed, 84

Satellite Launch Vehicle Programme, *see also* SLVP, 18
SEBI, *see also* Securities and Exchange Board of India, 73, 82
Securities and Exchange Board of India, *see also* SEBI, 73
Seven-Step Leadership Development Process, 89

Shaper, vii, ix, x, xii, xiii, xiv, xv, 5, 12, 45, 46, 47, 49, 51, 61, 72, 95, 96, 98, 109, 110, 111, 117, 119, 124, 125, 126, 127, 128, 129, 133, 134
shipbuilding, 7, 10, 83
SLVP, *see also* Satellite Launch Vehicle Programme, 19
smart city, 85
stock price determination, 67, 68
Subrahmanyan, 71
switchgear, 15, 16, 17

Tata, viii, 7, 8, 57, 106, 113
trading company, 6
transformational leadership, 95, 124
Tullow India, 78
TVS, viii

UTI, 69
Utkal Machinery Limited, 14, 15
Utmal, 15

value creation, xiii, xiv, 65, 68, 69, 71, 81, 98
Venkataramanan, 39, 47, 49,

50, 71, 72, 80, 86, 102, 104, 134

Welch, Jack, xiii, 21, 66, 73, 74, 97
white knight, 58

White Revolution, 11, 12, 13
Work–Life Integration, xiii, 104
World War I, 5
World War II, 5, 7, 9
Worli Dairy, 12